D0903667

THE LITURGICAL YEAR

joan chittister

THOMAS NELSON
Since 1798

NASHVILLE   DALLAS   MEXICO CITY   RIO DE JANEIRO   BEIJING

© 2009 by Joan Chittister

All rights reserved. No portion of this book may be reproduced, stored in a retrieval system, or transmitted in any form or by any means—electronic, mechanical, photocopy, recording, scanning, or other—except for brief quotations in critical reviews or articles, without the prior written permission of the publisher.

Published in Nashville, Tennessee, by Thomas Nelson. Thomas Nelson is a trademark of Thomas Nelson, Inc.

Page Design by Casey Hooper.

Thomas Nelson, Inc., titles may be purchased in bulk for educational, business, fund-raising, or sales promotional use. For information, please e-mail SpecialMarkets@ThomasNelson.com.

Unless otherwise noted, Scripture quotations are taken from the NEW REVISED STANDARD VERSION of the Bible. © 1989 by the Division of Christian Education of the National Council of the Churches of Christ in the U.S.A. All rights reserved.

Scriptures marked NKJV are taken from THE NEW KING JAMES VERSION. © 1982 by Thomas Nelson, Inc. Used by permission. All rights reserved.

Scriptures marked ESV are taken from THE ENGLISH STANDARD VERSION. © 2001 by Crossway Bibles, a division of Good News Publishers.

Scriptures marked KJV are taken from the King James Version of the Bible. Public domain.

Scriptures marked DRB are taken from the Douay-Rheims Bible. Public domain.

Library of Congress Cataloging-in-Publication Data

Chittister, Joan.
    The liturgical year / Joan Chittister.
      p. cm.
    Includes bibliographical references.
    ISBN 978-0-8499-0119-5 (hardcover)
    1. Church year. I. Title.
    BV30.C45 2009
    263'.9—dc22

2009007912

Printed in the United States of America
09 10 11 12 13 WC 7 6 5 4 3 2 1

This book is dedicated to liturgists everywhere,
and in a special way
to my Benedictine Sisters
Marilyn Schauble and Charlotte Zalot,
whose commitment to liturgical education
and liturgical planning
both freshens an ancient faith
and deepens the soul of the church.

CONTENTS

ACKNOWLEDGMENTS

IT IS NOT EASY TO ACKNOWLEDGE THE MULTIPLE consultations, discussions, models, and mentors that have been a lifetime in development in a subject like liturgical spirituality. After all, we grow from stage to stage, not in a straight line but in a circle, covering the same liturgical landscape over and over again as we go. The questions of who taught us what and when finally blur over time until eventually those concepts merge into one large, crazy quilt of ideas all within one border called "the spiritual life."

On the other hand, nothing on earth can be simpler to remember and easier to signify than the people whose lives, over the years, were instrumental in bringing us to the point of understanding the central and significant issues of our own.

In my own case, a monastic life lived in the context of the liturgical year brings with it the memory of a plethora of mentors in the field, whole categories of people, whose insights live on in me. This book, my own spirituality of the liturgical year, the layers of values and understandings I bring to every feast and season of the year, have been marked by each of them.

There were early childhood teachers, of course, who mapped out devotions that, in the end, defined the theological constructs of the year more clearly than any text-book ever could have done. They showed us manger scenes that taught us Christmas, for instance. They trained us in religious disciplines for Lent that taught us what it meant to develop self-control. They used Halloween to teach us the lives of the saints. They built "holy days" into the routine of our lives. They celebrated the great feasts of the church with special treats, colored vest-ments, and great displays of flowers and candles and incense that sweetened life with the sense of eternal mys-tery. Then, they lived the ordinariness of feria days with a stolidity of commitment that brooked no questions about the meaning of a life marked by both sorrow and joy. It was a parochial life lived under the daily influence of the church year, taught in the schools, followed in the home, expressed in the liturgies of the church.

Later, for those who went to a monastery as I did, for-mation directors deepened that work of a lifetime by sim-ply making us aware of the daily ebb and flow of the seasons. We learned, as novices, to mark our breviaries, to read the daily liturgical calendar with precision. They schooled us to reflect on the readings of the day and the feasts of the time. Because of them we learned to breathe the spirit of the seasons.

But most of all, it was liturgists and the liturgy itself that made the depths of the faith ever new, ever real to us.

Processions took us back to Golgotha and made us aware of the journeys of our own lives through darkness and depression. Vigils and song built up in us the great sense of anticipation that was Advent. They created liturgies that immersed the community in quiet. They slowed the pace of the community and plunged us into the increasing tension of Lent. They developed a liturgical life that was as much about life here and now and us as it was a rehearsal of the life and times of Jesus. They made the past present and the life of Jesus a breathing part of our own.

All of those people—teachers, families, pastors, parents, spiritual directors, and liturgists—in each of our lives, must be acknowledged as the shapers of our souls and the sharpeners of our inner vision. By inscribing the truths of the faith so forcefully on the routine of my own life, they have written on every page in this book. I am grateful for what each of them contributed to my lifetime of submergence in the tradition and in its recurring spiritual truths. Without those people, this book could never have been written. They are a prelude to its purpose.

But there are others whose relationship to this work is more immediate and no less steeped in the material than those who formed us all in the past. In this case, I am particularly indebted to those who contributed to these ideas and to those who did so much to bring this kind of work to light.

I am particularly indebted to Phyllis Tickle and Matt Baugher, the editorial framers of this series. By conceiving of the need to give continuing substance to the ongoing value and continual linkage between ancient devotions and a contemporary spiritual life, they make possible the spiritual formation of a generation to come. Their invitation to participate in the publication of this series has been one of the most spiritually enriching projects of my own professional life.

More than that, their vision and commitment to this series gives new energy to devotions and spiritual concepts that might otherwise have become passé in a technological and efficiency-centered world. Nothing can be further from the truth. To lose the substance of the liturgical tradition is to surrender even the spiritual life to the dangers of superficiality, to drain the faith of meaning, to deprive our lives of the ongoing presence of the living God.

Most of all, it is those liturgists who have guided the church through era after era of growth, development, and change, to whom we all owe a debt of gratitude for giving us both roots and wings in times when change, even spiritual change, to be successful, most needs the stabilizing effects of tradition.

Among the liturgical theorists whose work is clearly at the base of this work and the pastoral liturgists who commit themselves to the daily development of the rituals of every Christian denomination, I am indebted in a special way to Marilyn Schauble, OSB, and Charlotte Zalot, OSB, whose editorial discussions and intense attention to the manuscript brought both depth and meaning to the text. They have spent their adult professional lives teaching liturgy both to our Benedictine community and to the public. This book is a tribute to that kind of serious-minded commitment to the evolution of a theologically sound liturgical spirituality in the church.

I am also, of course, especially conscious of my continuing indebtedness to the sister-staff, whose skill and expertise make my work available to the public in a form that is both cogent and correct. Sisters Susan Doubet and Marlene Bertke did the hard work of preparing the manuscript for the publisher. Sister Maureen Tobin facilitated all of the contacts, calls, follow-up, and general communication needed to organize the numbers of people modern publishing involves. Their own lives of service and commitment make the meaning of community real and spiritual development true.

Finally, I would overlook the most telling of the tests of such a work if I failed to recognize those Christians who over the years and the centuries have become part of the liturgical life of Benedictine monasteries, my own included. They have come by the hundreds of thousands over the years as sign and proof of the meaning of liturgy in the lives of us all.

But then, why not? Without the liturgy, what does really bind the faith community together? Without the liturgical cycle, how shall we deepen our own personal understandings of what it means to live more fully, more deeply, more spiritually from year to year?

The liturgical life is not a relic of the past. It is the resounding reality of life in the present lived out of an ancient but living faith.

Whatever errors there are in this book, I own. Whatever insights there are in this book, I offer in recognition of those who, thank God, offered them first to me.

NOTE TO THE READER

FOR OBVIOUS REASONS, THIS WORK ON THE LITUR-
gical year is presented from the framework lived for centuries by the Roman Catholic community. For instance,
because I bring to the subject a life formed in a Roman
Catholic Benedictine monastery, it uses a Roman Catholic
liturgical calendar to explain the relation of one type of
feast to another. It uses the distinction between major feasts
and feria days, between Ordinary Time and Christmas or
Easter as it has developed in that church over the centuries.

Nevertheless, it is, at the end, simply one particular
template of a liturgical year that is common to all Christian
denominations. In some cases, it will reveal itself in the
use of language: Catholics talk about "feast days," for
instance, and mean celebrations. We divide feasts under
the categories of "major" and "minor" feasts to distinguish between greater or lesser celebrations. We carry
with us some Latin names for what are now very contemporary events, like the Triduum, referring to the three
days that are the height of Holy Week—Holy Thursday,
Good Friday, and Holy Saturday. But however the
Catholic tradition may reveal itself here, it is not this specific template that is important to this book. It is the
liturgical poles of the Christian life—Christmas and

Easter—that are common to us all that is the real content of the work.

It is the nature of liturgical spirituality itself—the attempt to live the Jesus life over and over again all the years of our lives—that is of the essence of this book. It is about the spirituality of joy and suffering, of waiting and faith, of asceticism and celebration, of loss and hope that marks all our lives and that needs to be strengthened, deepened, revisited, and rediscovered in the life of Jesus and the life of the church every year of our lives.

My hope is that this overview of the spiritual dimensions of the liturgical year will be a gift to the whole Christian family as we learn from one another the way to find God here, to follow Jesus always, and to live in the footsteps of the ancients who have handed on to us the liturgical traditions that nourish our souls and soften our hearts as we go.

FOREWORD

IF THERE IS ANY ONE THING THAT CHARACTERIZES Western Christianity in our times, it most certainly is a kind of yearning—a kind of keening need, actually—to see and know and feel and touch again that from which we have come.

The centuries between us and the original disciples and apostles and converts who were and are our forebears in the faith have not always been kind to us, their progeny. Over the intervening centuries, family disagreements that ran the gamut from theological squabbles to armed, internecine battles have barred us from access to many of our rightful treasures and, thereby, have robbed us of many of the physical evidences of our common heritage. Occasionally, even, a rupture has been so cataclysmic as to take away the very memory of those lost heirlooms of worship and faithful formation.

Now, however, we live in a globalizing world of increasing contact among all of the people of God as well as of an expanding base of information about the centuries of Christian time behind us. And from within that new world of knowing, we long to know as well—and with an appropriating intimacy—the ways and wisdom of the church in the years it still worshipped with those who had known the

Lord, or those who had known those who had known Him in earthly time. We ask ourselves questions about how Christ worshipped while He was here and why, about how He taught His disciples to worship and in what context. We ask as well about how they adapted as their own changing circumstances rolled on into the decades of the second and then the third centuries of our common era.

We ask, because we sense both intuitively and rationally that somewhere along the way, we have wandered too far from home, too far from the center of common practice and common confession that informed Him and them. Where we have gone and what we have become in our variations and diversity is alive but somehow incomplete. Like lovely flowers scattered on a tabletop, we see ourselves as less than a gathering and our beauty as less than that of a full bouquet. We seek the vessel that will contain and support and nourish us in our shared faith as well as in our individual beauty. The Ancient Practices series is about that search. That is, it is about the ancient practices that by birthright are the unifying and nourishing vessel of the church.

The ancient practices of the faith are seven in number, have come into Christianity out of Judaism, and inform all of the Abrahamic faiths. Three of them—tithing, fasting, and the sacred meal—have to do with the physical body, its work and its needs. Three of them have to do with the monitoring of time. Fixed-hour prayer regulates the hours of the day, and Sabbath-keeping monitors the days of the week. The liturgical year monitors or paces those same days and the weeks into the cohesive whole of basic human timekeeping, the year itself. The seventh of them, pilgrimage, engages both the physical space of the body and the dimension of time, requiring that we go at least once in a lifetime with holy intention to a place made sacred by the faith and encounters of other believers.

This book, as is clear from its title, is about the sixth discipline, the liturgical year. This is the third and greatest of the time-governing practices. It is also, along with fixed-hour prayer, one of the two most difficult of the practices to approach.

Whatever the shape, form, or variation of Christianity one may adhere to in the West, there is always some recognition that a day of rest or Sabbath exists; that tithing (or some form of giving) is expected; that Communion (or Eucharist or the Lord's Supper or the Mass) is part of our faith in some more or less central or generally acknowledged way; that fasting can be anything from a superficial conversation-maker to a dangerous denial and back again; and that a pilgrimage can be beneficial to one's psyche as well as body and soul. Fixed-hour prayer, however, and the observation of the liturgical year both have a different cachet.

For one thing, fixed-hour prayer and the liturgical year are unrelentingly in one's face every day. There is no escaping either of them. In addition—and herein lies the real rub, I suspect—they both require a certain amount of intellectual commitment or awareness and/or just plain information. Unfortunately, that mix of requirements is even truer for the liturgical year than it is for fixed-hour prayer. Yet it is the liturgical year that most consistently houses, and unendingly transmits to us, the full scope and play of our Christian-ness. It is the liturgical year that gears our rhythms and courses to that of the church everywhere in all times, present and past, and all places, here and otherwise. It is the observance of the liturgical year that tells over and over again through all the years of our lives the Story that informs us and that we are fulfilling.

Sr. Joan Chittister, much-loved author and counselor and fond voice across all the divisions of Christendom, is uniquely—I would argue, providentially—positioned to talk to us about the centrality of the liturgical year to our practice as individual Christians and as the church. A Benedictine by profession, she has lived the liturgical year with faithfulness for all of her own physical ones and, as a result, has learned to hold its observation and governances in both affection and respectful awe. What Sr. Joan gives us in her discussion here is part historical instruction, part Christian mentoring, and part gentle wisdom. Nowhere, though, is she in the business of persuading us— she's far too seasoned a believer for that.

Rather, Sr. Joan would have us engage with affection and comfort the questions about what this particular gift from the fathers and mothers of the faith really is. Only after we have done that can any one of us hope to discern where, in the coursings of our lives, this practice may or may not inform us to our soul's benefit.

So, in Sr. Joan's name and at her behest, I invite you to read *The Liturgical Year*. Admittedly, I fervently pray that none of us will ever be the same again, once we are done with our reading.

Phyllis Tickle
General Editor,
Ancient Practice Series

1

THE SPIRALING ADVENTURE OF THE SPIRITUAL LIFE

LIFE IS MADE UP OF THE TURNING OF THE YEARS. WE watch our lives go by, a phase, a stage, a year at a time, and we mark the meaning of the year by the way we feel as we spend it. We talk about "the kind of year it's been." As if one year could possibly repeat another, as if all the parts of the year were cut from the same fabric, all its days derived from the same root or developed in the same ways. Instead, every year is a distinct growth point in life, the shedding of another shell of life. Each year brings something unique to us and calls for something different from us. Yet, however much we recognize their separate comings and goings, we, too, often neglect to be prepared for their equally unique effects on our development.

More than that, so often we fail to realize that any

given year can be many years in one—the year he got married, the year she graduated from college, the year the child died—each facet of it a separate and discrete reality in itself. No doubt about it: as life inches on, the truth of the spiritual uniqueness of every year becomes more and more apparent. There is no such thing as a universal year, a simple rendering of a common block of time. There are actually a good many ways, not only one, by which to define the years of our lives. So many, in fact, that it's important that we take pains not to confuse one kind of year with another.

> *Every year is a distinct growth point in life,*
> *the shedding of another shell of life.*

Every different kind of year demands different strengths of us, provides different kinds of gifts for us, enables different kinds of sensibilities in us. To confuse one kind of year with another, then, is to assume that they are all equally valuable or that we can possibly achieve all the things we need in life—material or spiritual—in any single one of them. Nothing could be further from the truth.

The years of our lives come in more flavors than any single year can possibly encompass. There are, in fact, a good many kinds of years by which we shape our work, our family life, our very selves. To fail to distinguish one kind of year from another is to risk skewing the way we look at life. The way we define our years determines what we think our lives are meant to be about and how we will live because of it. There are fiscal years and school years, planting periods and harvesting periods, calendar years and business years. There are years to mark every stage of life—childhood, adolescence, adulthood, middle age, and old age—and all of those periods are unlike the periods before it. The question is, what kind of year means the most to us spiritually? What in the spiritual life is there to enable us to live all of the other years well, to their fullness, to the elastic limits of our growing souls?

I began writing this book on New Year's Day, the first day of the amount of time it will take for the earth to revolve around the sun again. But the fact that I began to write about the meaning and character of the Christian year on the day the civic year began was a matter of pure coincidence. Ironically enough, the fact that it was the beginning of another calendar year had nothing whatsoever to do with the subject matter of this book.

I am writing about the Christian year, the liturgical year, the year that puts in relief the full array of Christian mysteries and spiritual cycles for all to see. But unlike the civic year, the Christian year does not begin on January 1. The church year begins on the first Sunday of Advent, which normally begins in late November. The point is clear: many periods of time shape us, and most of them do not begin or end at the same time.

This book, then, does not concentrate simply on what it means to grow older as one year succeeds another. This book is about growing wiser, growing holier, growing more embedded in the essentials of life as the years go by rather than simply moving from one time of life to the next. The liturgical year is an adventure in bringing the Christian life to fullness, the heart to alert, the soul to focus. It does not concern itself with the questions of how to make a living. It concerns itself with the questions of how to make a life.

> *The liturgical year is an adventure in bringing the Christian life to fullness, the heart to alert, the soul to focus.*

The truth is, then, that as Christians, January 1 isn't really our "new year" at all. It is not the beginning of the "new year" of our soul's search for wholeness. Instead, January 1 is simply the day that makes it possible for the secular world to mark centuries, to keep track of its earthly ways, to coordinate itself with the ways of the rest of the world, to begin again its cycle of civic events.

Other than that, the Christian year and the civic year go wafting by each other, often unaware, sometimes completely distinct in their measures of value and their indications of what is really important in life and what is not. To be a Christian is to see the deep-down difference between the two. And to celebrate that.

The civic new year is clearly only one of many "years" we all live, for one reason or another, with one emphasis or another, every year of our lives. Depending on who we are and what we do, we can live fiscal years and family years, school years and retirement years, apprentice years and professional years, one after another or even simultaneously, as our lives go by. All of them, though different, say something to us about what's determining in life, what's formative in life, what's meaningful to us in the here and now of life.

The civic new year is, at best, a calendrical device designed to regulate the daily affairs of a people. It enables people to count time together—three weeks until we leave for the next trip, for instance; or to plot future engagements, such as the date on which we will close the deal on the new house, to mark the weekend of the next meeting, or to calculate the time when we can all expect snow again. The civic new year as we know it is a purely solar event, a chart of the planet's journey around the sun. But it is not, except in the most private and personal of ways, the story of the rest of us, the narrative of our spiritual lives. That story begins and ends and begins again annually with the journey of the soul through the liturgical year, the year that marks the major moments in Christian spirituality and so points our own lives in the same direction.

The liturgical year is the year that sets out to attune the life of the Christian to the life of Jesus, the Christ. It proposes, year after year, to immerse us over and over again into the sense and substance of the Christian life until, eventually, we become what we say we are—followers of Jesus all the way to the heart of God. The liturgical year is an adventure in human growth, an exercise in spiritual ripening.

It wasn't always that for me. For long years, the liturgical life as I learned it was simply a round of fast days and feast days, arranged by who-knew-whom for the sake of who-knew-what. Some of them delighted me, all of them fascinated me, but few of them had much to say to me in those early days about the purpose of my life. I'm older now; I know better now. I know now that it is possible to grow physically older by the day but, at the same time, stay spiritually juvenile, if our lives are not directed by a schema far beyond the march of our planet around the sun.

Like the rings on a tree, the cycles of Christian feasts are meant to mark the levels of our spiritual growth from one stage to another in the process of human growth. They add layer after layer to the meaning of life, to the sense of what it entails to live beyond the immediate and into the significant dimensions of human existence. The seasons and feasts, the fasts and solemnities, if we are open and alert to them, lead us deeper and deeper into the self, beyond the pull of the present, higher and higher into the One who beckons us on through time to that moment when we will dissolve into God, set free from time to become one with the universe.

> *Like the rings on a tree, the cycles of Christian feasts are meant to mark the levels of our spiritual growth from one stage to another in the process of human growth.*

The secret lies in coming to understand the Christian year so that it might work its cosmic dimensions of what it means to be alive right into the fiber of our daily lives.

This book sets out to open what may at first seem to be an arbitrary arrangement of ancient holy days or liturgical seasons to their essential relationship to one another and their ongoing meaning to us. It is an excursion into life from the Christian perspective, from the viewpoint of those who set out not only to follow Jesus but to live as Jesus lived, to think as Jesus thought, to become what Jesus had become by the end of His life.

It is the presentation of the Christian mysteries and their eternal place in life, both in His life and ours as well. It is a book about the journey of the soul through the map of Christian time.

This book will not only explore the major seasons and feasts of the church as they developed in the past but will consider their place in our own spiritual development in the present.

This book is not merely about the past. It is not limited to past events in the life of Christ or historical problems in the lives of ancient saints. It is also about what it takes to live a spiritual life now that is as rich and as meaningful in this day and age as it was for those who preceded us in all the eons of the Christian tradition.

We follow Jesus, we say. But what does that mean? How do we know if that's really true or not? And in what way does such a thing as "the church year" provide both an insight into what it means to follow Christ and the support to do that?

This book is about the role of the church year in bringing each of us to a fuller understanding of the Christian life—and, most of all, it is about explaining precisely what it means to live a Christian life.

2

A LIVING MODEL,
A REAL LIFE

SOME YEARS AGO, COMMENTATORS REPORTED WITH a kind of muted disbelief that a U.S. governor had ordered a prisoner on death row removed from terminal treatment at a local hospital and returned on a gurney to the state prison in order to execute him on the appointed date. No flexibility, no mercy, no more physical care. In the same vein, British immigration officers years later removed Ama Sumani, a thirty-nine-year-old mother of two whose visa had lapsed, from treatment in a London hospital in order to deport her to Ghana. In Ghana, the same kind of dialysis was not available at any price. In both cases, the death sentence was clear and cold. At the same time, the spiritual question was equally direct: though legal, was either action really, authentically, truly Christian? What is the spiritual answer to such situations?

And how does the Christian decide? Does mercy ever trump law?

If the liturgical year is understood as it is supposed to be—the church's proclamation, lodestar, and participation in the life of Christ—then it is, at very least, the place a Christian can go to begin to determine the answers to questions such as these. Pope Pius XI, ardent thinker and author of thirty encyclicals between 1922 and 1939, called the liturgical year "the principal organ of the ordinary magisterium of the church."[1] The language may seem foreign to many of us now, but the ideas are not. In other words, the liturgical year is one of the teaching dimensions of the church. It is a lesson in life.

> *The liturgical year is one of the teaching dimensions of the church. It is a lesson in life.*

From the liturgy we learn both the faith and Scripture, both our ideals and our spiritual tradition. The cycle of Christian mysteries is wise teacher, clear model, and recurring and constant reminder of the Christ-life in our midst. Simply by being itself over and over again, simply by putting before our eyes and filtering into our hearts the living presence of the Jesus who walked from Galilee to Jerusalem doing good, it teaches us to do the same. As Jesus lived, despite either the restrictions or the regulations of His age, so, the liturgical year teaches us, must we.

In the liturgy, then, is the standard of what it means to live a Christian life both as the church and as individuals. The seasons and cycles and solemnities put before us in the liturgical year are more than representations of time past; they are an unending sign—a veritable sacrament of life. It is through them that the Christ-life becomes present in our own lives in the here and now.

It is in the liturgy that we meet the Jesus of history and come to understand the Christ of faith who is with us still.

The point is, at one level, a rather shocking one. Can the spiritual life possibly be that simple? And yet the point becomes even less ambiguous as the years go by: the liturgical year, we come to realize, is the cry of the centuries to every new age neither to forget nor to forsake the vision of the first Christian age or the challenges of this one. It is, in fact, the life of Jesus that really guides the church through time. It is the life of Jesus that judges the conduct of the time. It is the life of Jesus that is the standard of the souls who call themselves Christian in every age, however seductive the errors of the age itself.

In every age, the liturgical year exists to immerse its world in the current as well as the eternal meanings of the Christian life.

Then, after years of repeating the messages of the

feasts and probing their meanings for our own lives, we come to a point where we look back over the decades and realize that little by little the slow drip, drip, drip of the Christian ideal has insinuated itself into the deepest parts of our psyches. We, who squirmed through Lent as children and stood only half aware through long Easter readings as young adults, who wore Ash Wednesday's ashes with equal parts of pride and embarrassment as adult sophisticates, become conscious as the years go by of the tendrils of hope and desire, of commitment and conviction such practices have rooted in our hearts. We come to know ourselves to be more than simply an empty self. We come to know ourselves to be Christian.

As the self dissolves into Christ, we come to see ourselves as one people together and, at the same time, distinct persons who have developed clear and common attitudes toward the rest of life. We come to realize that we have gained this perspective almost unconsciously from the life of the just and compassionate Jesus, who slipped quietly into our minds in the course of the relentless repetition of the liturgical year. Now we know why we are bothered by the sight of a man carried from a hospital given to saving lives to a prison dedicated to extinguishing them. We come to understand why we turned away uncomfortable from a television interview with a helpless woman who would soon be taken off dialysis to die in her impoverished country of origin because her visa had run out in the one that had the resources to save her.

The liturgical year is the process of slow, sure immersion in the life of Christ that, in the end, claims us, too, as heralds of that life ourselves.

The continuing proclamation of the Scriptures, the centrality of the Gospels as the foundation of every liturgy, and the ongoing reflection on those readings in homilies year after year do two things: one of them communal, the other personal.

First, the liturgical year reminds us as the church what kind of a community we are meant to be. It convicts us as the church of the betrayal of those ideals when we are not a voice in the face of holocaust or not the protectors of its children. Then we must all repent and begin again.

> *The liturgical year reminds us as the church*
> *what kind of a community we are meant to be.*

Second, the liturgical year implants within each of us individually the reprise of those moments that are the substance of the faith. It calls us to face the distance between the ideals we see in the life of Christ and the pale ghost of them we find in our own. It calls us to private and personal reflection on the place of Jesus in the daily exercise of our existence.

The liturgical year, then, is the lodestar, the Polaris, of what we are really seeking when we say we seek the "good" or argue that our efforts are "worthy" of what we mean when we call ourselves Christian.

Finally, the liturgical year presents us with the standard of participation in the Christian life that we must bring to the spiritual life both to be called Christian as well as to become Christian.

The liturgical year is not an idle discipline, not a sentimentalist's definition of piety, not an historical anachronism. It is Jesus with us, for us, and in us as we strive to make His life our own. It is goad and guide to the kind of personal spirituality that is worthy of the Jesus whose commitment to the Word of God led Him all the way to the cross and beyond it—to Resurrection.

> *The liturgical year . . . is Jesus with us, for us,*
> *and in us as we strive to make His life our own.*

It is, without doubt, learning to live the liturgical year that makes a difference to every other year of our lives.

3

THE YEAR THAT GIVES MEANING TO EVERY OTHER YEAR

THE WOMAN WHO TOLD ME THE STORY NEVER doubted the truth of it for a moment. Fighting sleep at the wheel of a car one night, she said, she heard her mother's voice—sharp and piercing—shouting her name. Just as the car veered to the edge of the mountain road's over-hang, she jerked awake, wrenched the car away from the edge of the cliff, and saved her life. "I know my mother's voice," the woman said simply. "I know she was with me."

In the Christian heart, just as the voice of a mother long dead goes on ringing in the ear—a living sign of ongoing relationship and direction, even if from another dimension—so does the life of Christ go on animating the church. Nowhere more than in the liturgical year is that presence felt and seen and heard. It calls to us in the commemoration of the mysteries. It awakens us in the words of the liturgy. It rouses us with the lives of the saints. It rallies in us the awareness that the ordinariness of our own life is a link to the meaning of the life of Jesus for us in the rest of the year.

No doubt about it: the liturgical year is the arena where our life and the life of Jesus intersect. In no other spiritual practice is that presence of Jesus so searing, so personal, so clear, so developmental, so immediate. It is what that presence means to us now, in this life of ours, in this world of ours, that the liturgical year is really all about. In the liturgical year we walk with Jesus through all the details of His life—and He walks with us in ours.

> *The liturgical year is the arena where our*
> *life and the life of Jesus intersect.*

This awareness of the dynamic relationship between the life of Jesus and the life of the Christian community, between the individual Christian life and the Jesus life, both past and present—emerges early in the church. Early Christians knew without doubt that all facets of the life of Christ stemmed from one reality, were related to one reality, led to one reality, were aspects of one central reality: the cross. Jesus was born to confront the cross; Jesus died on the cross to bring us to fullness of life; Jesus rose to defeat the cross; Jesus embodied what the role of the cross was to be in the life of us all. Clearly, it was the reality of the cross that defined the life of Jesus, the Christ. And it is the reality of the cross that defines the life of the individual Christian, both then and now.

It was on the cross during Passover, the Jewish feast commemorating the journey from death to life of an Israel enslaved in Egypt, that Jesus paid the price for being what the world could not recognize or, worse, did not want: the voice of God, the fulfillment of the Law. Then, the Jewish slaughter of the lambs in memory of the great Exodus from Egypt and the death of Jesus, the new Lamb of God, became forever the same, forever distinct. It was on the cross that Jesus, the new Moses, led the people through a desert of darkened understanding from one insight into the will of God for them to another.

But it was not the glorification of suffering that characterized the early Christian community. On the contrary, this was a community filled with new life. It was exactly the liberation from death on the cross that came with Jesus' resurrection that marked the meaning of the Christian life for all time. Jesus risen becomes the animating life of the Christian community. The life of Jesus, once a prophetic voice in a troubled world, became in death the prophetic promise of new life to come.

The consciousness of Jesus as the fullness of the mind

of God for the world not only changed the Jewish community, it changed the world itself. Now life could no longer be imagined as simply a brief and empty moment on the world stage, largely without consequence, wholly without meaning. The life of the Jesus we follow had been brief—and world shaking. It was, if anything, a sign to us of our own place in the scheme of things, in the order of the universe, in the economy of salvation. Now, it was clear, every capacity for good, every effort of anyone, every breath of every human being had significance. Now, we saw in Jesus, the grave was not the end, God was not remote, life was not purposeless, and the individual was not nothing.

The life and death of Jesus gave promise of the deliverance of the human condition. Because Jesus lived the very life we live, He identified with the eternal worth and lasting import of every single one of us. Jesus' life on earth was the thunderous acclamation of a living God that every hair on the human head was not only counted but it had meaning. It was precious to its Maker. It had a purpose beyond itself. Now it became obvious: if the life of Christ was to continue here on earth, it must continue in us. Such an astonishingly piercing assessment of who Jesus really was and what that implies for those who call themselves Christian constituted a momentous breakthrough in the human awareness of the panoptic significance of the individual spiritual life.

> *Because Jesus lived the very life we live, He identified with the*
> *eternal worth and lasting import of every single one of us.*

And so the liturgical year, the daily immersion of the Christian community in the illuminating life of Jesus, in the mystery of God's will and the power of God's presence, came to be. Accounts of pilgrimages to Jerusalem in the early fourth century, for instance, describe in great detail the commemoration of the Passion of Christ there. Nothing is forgotten, minimized, or overlooked in the process. Every spot associated with the life and death of Jesus is now understood to be a holy spot; every site is a place of sacred origin: Egeria, a pilgrim of the fifth century who kept a diary of liturgical events in the Christian community there during Passover, reports the places that marked the life and Passion of Jesus. In recording the sacred stations and readings of the early Christian community, she preserved them for centuries to come and made them important to us yet.[1] It is a liturgy of life—Jesus' life and our own—that we are about in the Passion liturgies.

Each element of the Passion has something to say to our own lives and time as well. Jerusalem and the final Passover meal among the apostles includes for their personal reflection—and so for ours—the notion that the spiritual leader is to be more servant than Lord. Golgotha, with its memory of the betrayal by people who, once blessed by Jesus, now discovered more politically profitable motives elsewhere, is an eternal reminder of the pain of abandonment. The tomb where they laid Him, empty when they returned, becomes the thundering challenge to the Christian's understanding of the end of life. Bethlehem, the small village venerated since the third century as the site of the Nativity becomes, in the liturgy, universally significant. And, finally, the Mount of Olives, revered now as the site of His Ascension to that place beyond the earth where everything earthly will someday find itself whole and complete, accomplished and fulfilled, lifts our own sights to life beyond this one.

Thanks to the diary of Egeria, every moment in the life of Christ is marked by liturgical meaning. They were real in the fifth century, and they are still real in our own. Every sacred site on this ancient pilgrimage about the unfolding of the life of Jesus is noted, is revered, is remembered for its depth of meaning, not simply to the life of Jesus but to the life of the contemporary church as well. No segment of the journey to the cross is forgotten. Every step of it is simply one more step between the ways of God with us in our ancestral past and the will of God for us now. Every step on the way to the fullness of God's plan for us all, the Christian knows, has been foretold; every step has been finished. Except, of course, for our own. And it is Jesus as the link between past and present who, in the liturgical year, is its substance for each of us.

Now we recognize that if Jesus' life is to have eternal impact in the Christian community and beyond, it will depend on our being part of the mystery ourselves. We must pray our way into it. We must think our way into it. We must live our way into it.

The historical development of the liturgical year has been a slow one, of course, tempered by time, dependent on circumstances, variable in small dimensions from age to age but always clear on one point: the purpose of the liturgical year is to bring to life in us and around us, little by little, one layer of insight after another until we grow to full stature in the spiritual life. Intent on living a spiritual life that matters rather than a spiritual fad that fascinates or a spiritual program that anesthetizes the soul to everything but the self, we find out in the liturgy what makes life matter by following Jesus through every element of it.

> *The purpose of the liturgical year is to bring to life in us and around us, little by little, one layer of insight after another until we grow to full stature in the spiritual life.*

Like the voices of loved ones gone before us, the liturgical year is the voice of Jesus calling to us every day of our lives to wake our sleeping selves from the drowsing

effects of purposelessness and meaninglessness, material-
ism and hedonism, rationalism and indifference, to attend
to the life of the Jesus who cries within us for fulfillment.

When that happens, then the world will change. Then
the people will be saved. Then the reign of God promised
by Jesus, preached by the apostles, and proclaimed by the
lives of the saints will have come. Then life will be what it
is meant to be: the love of God fully alive in us.

4

THE COMPONENTS OF THE LITURGICAL YEAR

THE LITURGICAL YEAR MARKS THE CHRISTIAN community as Christian, true. But it takes more than simply keeping the liturgical rules and regulations, or celebrating feast days and fast days all lined up in a row, to claim we have lived the year well and so can really be called Christian. The liturgical year is the process of coming back year after year to look at what we already know, on one level, but are newly surprised by again and again: Did He, this Jesus, really die that we might all understand that life is bigger than systems and more important than kings, that there is something more to life than we can see? Is that all there is to it? Is the point of the whole thing simply that we must live our lives—magnetized by what we cannot be sure of but do surely know—as a beacon to others of the presence of God? What else could it be?

To live the liturgical year is to keep our lives riveted on one beam of light called the death and Resurrection of Jesus and its meaning for us here and now. One. Just one.

But if the entire liturgical year, if the life of every Christian, is dedicated to one major moment, and one moment only, to the death and Resurrection of Jesus, then why so many other celebrations and memorials, solemnities and seasons during the year? Why not just one celebration, one liturgical season, one great feast? What are we to think about all those other days children remember for their incense and their flowers, their choirs and organs, their ecclesiastical splendor and the crush of the worshipping crowds?

> *To live the liturgical year is to keep our lives riveted*
> *on one beam of light called the death and Resurrection*
> *of Jesus and its meaning for us here and now.*

The questions are important ones. After all, who among us doesn't remember a great deal more churchgoing in their lives than one single feast can possibly explain? There are memories, for instance, of the long weeks of purple vestments or covered statues that preceded Christmas and Easter. There are the family pictures of altar servers and flower girls, of choirboys and page boys in solemn procession up and down church aisles and around city blocks while incense curled around their heads. There is the now dimming recollection of the strewing of flowers, the ringing of bells as bishops and priests led the assembly in the celebration of the feast of Corpus Christi or Trinity Sunday or the crowning of Mary, Queen of the May. What about all of these other feast days? Where did they come from? Where are they now? And what do they have to do with the great feast?

Even now, years after the liturgical renewal of the 1950s, the signs and signals of a faith rich in insights and embedded in tradition are many. Advent calendars line the walls of churches and religious education classrooms; Lenten boxes call for sacrifice in behalf of needy others; Alleluias are sung or not sung, depending on the time of year, the nature of a feast day, and the character of the season.

No, the liturgical year is clearly not one single moment in time. It is many moments in time—all of them coming together, all of them leading us to one energizing, everlasting center of reality: the memory of the cross and the meaning of Resurrection, both for Jesus and for ourselves. It is the beginning of new life in us.

The liturgical year, then, is a panoply, an array of events designed to shape us into being what we say we are—followers of Jesus, disciples of Christ, the Christian community. It is a yearlong sojourn through the life of Christ to that ultimate point of self-giving, to that last breath of teaching, to that total surrender to the will of God, to that glorious new life that comes when we put this one at its service.

The liturgical year, then, is a panoply, an array of events designed to shape us into being what we say we are— followers of Jesus, disciples of Christ, the Christian community.

The church year is not the marking of one luculent, passing moment in the midst of eleven long months of dark nothingness all the rest of the year. It is month after month, every year of our lives, being taken back to the empty cross and the empty tomb, one way or another, in order to shape our own life in the light of them. It is those moments that reiterate the core of the faith. They re-echo the call of our lives. They point us with spiritual clarity toward those laserlike events in which everything we say we believe is tested, becomes real, becomes total, becomes the light of Christ for all to see—this time in us.

Anything else is empty ritual, pure religious display, pomp without purpose.

It is what the cross and tomb demand of our own lives as well as what they meant for Jesus that makes the liturgical year more than theater, more than memory, more than history, more than cult. It is what the feast days and seasons, saints days and cycles tell us about how to live life ourselves, how to make life meaningful, that make the liturgical year a catechesis as well as a celebration, a spiritual adventure as well as a liturgical exercise.

The liturgical year is the calendar of the spiritual life, the epicenter of the soul's progress through time. It punctuates our civic year with the mystery of who we are really meant to become. It is far beyond anything civic. It is greater than the culture of any single group. It transcends everybody's nationality. It reminds us of roots deeper than time and stronger than tribe. It never lets us sink into a kind of secular historicism that makes color or nationality or race or politics or gender the ultimate dimension of our lives. Instead, all the undercurrents of our existence are here: what we believe, who we follow, why we do what we do, and—in the end—where we're going.

To live the liturgical year well is to live down into the center of the soul. It denies us the right to run away from the self. It refuses us the option of fooling ourselves into believing that we are yet whole. It graces us with the awareness that the self is not the only dimension of our lives.

To do this, the liturgical year immerses the Christian in the life and death of Jesus from multiple perspectives. It invites us to walk with the Jesus of the Gospels, hearing what His followers heard, seeing what His followers saw. We see the Jesus who confronted the systems of His time. It gives us clear and common models of what it means to live a Christian life here and now. It shows us the Jesus who stops by the side of the road to heal the sick, parley with the outcast, and consort with foreigners. It engrafts us into the very lived experiences of searching for God and working for change and growing in truth that mark the development of the Christian life in all of us. And finally, it enables us to reflect on the major meanings of the faith, on the implications of what kind of god the God of Jesus really is.

To do all of this, the liturgical year steeps us in four major kinds of celebrations. First, we celebrate Sundays. In the earliest days of Christianity, only Sundays—"the little Easter"[1] or weekly remembrance of the death and Resurrection of Jesus—marked the Christian community as other than the Jewish community out of which it had sprung.

Second, we celebrate the seasons of the year. Of the two major seasons—Advent, before Christmas; and Lent, before Easter—Advent was the later development. The earliest evidence of the celebration of Christmas does not appear until the third century in Egypt. It was not common in the universal church until almost four centuries after the celebration of Lent and Easter.[2] On the other hand, the Christian community stood rooted in Easter, the Pasch, from the very beginning. On these two hinges, the birth of Jesus and the death of Jesus, hang the Christian view of life. Jesus came to show the world the will of the living God, and He died at the hands of a world that failed to recognize and accept it. The call of the Christian is to participate in the ongoing mission of Jesus.

Third, the sanctoral cycle, the commemorations of individuals noted for living out of the kind of personal holiness they saw in Jesus, leaves us the footprints of the faithful who have gone before us. This commemoration of models of the Christian life developed in a kind of higgledy-piggledy manner. Not all the feast days that accrued to the church calendar in early centuries were well-grounded spiritually or well-authenticated historically. Many of them were more political or social in origin than they were spiritual. But whatever the circumstances of their emergence, there they stand across the centuries, saying to each of us, *You can, like these, live it too. You can also, as this one did, make the life of Christ, marked by this year, celebrated by this community, your own.*

Ordinary Time—the two periods of time between Eastertide and Advent, and then again between Christmastide and Lent—translates the life of Jesus into the very marrow of life itself. With its punctuation of the sanctifying dailiness of life with "idea feasts," the great, solemn commemorations of great, solemn ideas like the Feast of the Trinity or the Feast of the Sacred Heart, it serves to teach major concepts of a faith that, ultimately, is rooted in the ongoing presence of Christ in the human community today.

Each of these periods, with its distinct types of celebration, develops a special depth of liturgical spirituality
in us. Each calls us to remember and be grateful for what
God's grace has done for us. The important thing to bear
in mind is that to celebrate any of them means a great
deal more than simply being consciously aware of their
place in Christian history. Every liturgical celebration is
far more than the historical commemoration of some past
period or place in time.

When we celebrate a feast of the liturgical year, we are
living out a special occasion on several distinct levels.
First, we are making the past present in a new way.
Second, we are making a public declaration of truth
about the life of Jesus and its meaning for us now. Third,
we are participating as a people in a communal amen to
what is a private as well as a public certainty about what
it means to be Christian. We are, moreover, reaffirming to
ourselves and to the world of our own time what being
Christian demands and what our personal and our public
life should be or must become. It is our common declaration that as individuals, as Christians, we will go on trying
to make it so.

Celebrating the liturgies of the liturgical year puts the
world on notice that we are Christians and we take the
meaning of the year and all its parts seriously.

Celebrating the liturgies of the liturgical year puts the world on notice that we are Christians and we take the meaning of the year and all its parts seriously.

To live the liturgical year is to remember God's goodness in life, day after day, week after week, season after season, and to remind ourselves ceaselessly, therefore, of our own obligation to live life differently as a result.

5

SUNDAY

PERHAPS THE FIRST CLEAR AND CERTAIN MEMORY OF religion in the human psyche—the awareness that religion, an institutionalized and formal immersion in God is a life-changing, world-changing event—comes early in life. At least it did for me.

Everywhere I went as a child in small-town USA, Sunday descended like a soft aura of unearthliness. Life was different on Sundays. Quiet set in. People stayed home. Traffic disappeared. Stores closed. Business windows went dark. The whole world felt blank, felt tentative, felt pregnant with anticipation. Then, out of nowhere, with no warning, bells began to peal. And everywhere you looked, people could be seen hurrying up great, wide, sweeping cement steps, streaming into churches on every corner. Indeed, Sunday was distinct from every other day of the week. Any child could see that. On Sundays, something unseen, something cosmic happened.

Even now, in a world gone computerized, gone globalized, gone mad, Sunday mornings have a taste of otherness about them. For Christians, Sundays arrive like moments out of time, bringing, in their invisible mist, the sight of another way to be human. The question is, why does this happen? What is there in us that draws us to recognize the spiritual parts of life, the very elements that make the material parts of life worthwhile? For the Christian, the relationship is a clear one.

> *For Christians, Sundays arrive like moments out of time, bringing, in their invisible mist, the sight of another way to be human.*

Sunday, to the Christian mind, is a "little Easter." It is the collective memory of the moment when the tomb opened, empty of the death it promised, and new life began. It is the moment when the Christian community remembers together again that death does not triumph, that evil cannot prevail, that the death of the spirit is not final, and that Jesus lives yet—in us. We know that we are called to be a new people. We are the people of the new beginning. We have the right to say no to despair because we have the right to say yes to hope in the One who shattered the darkness of life with the light of eternity. It is that very nourishment of the spirit on which the spirit depends.

Like Muslims on Friday and the Jewish community on Saturday, Christians, too, gather together weekly as a community on Sunday. On Sundays we give common voice to our gratitude to God for the Life that gives life within us. Then, renewed in that spirit, we commit ourselves as a people to go on building the world God intends for us all. Sunday after Sunday, Christians celebrate the fullness of life intended for us on all the other days and already begun in our life in Jesus.

But why Sunday? Why not some other day of the week? And what does Sunday mean to us now, all these generations later?

The sacred place of Sunday worship in Christian history has a more complex and tangled past than might at first be imagined. The dedication of Sunday as a day of Christian assembly, after all, came out of the Jewish community. Still thinking of themselves as Sabbath people, the followers of Jesus also knew that they were coming to know themselves as more than that. These were those who were waiting for a Messiah, yes, but who also knew now that they had seen Him among them. Risen. Translucent. Different.

This was a Messiah who said He had not come to change "one jot or one tittle" of the Law (Matt. 5:18 KJV). This was the Jesus who had also raised the Jewish cup of thanksgiving at the end of the Passover meal, and just before His own life had been sacrificed, said, "Do this in remembrance of me" (Luke 22:19). It was a memory burned into the minds of those who had not only followed Jesus to the cross but had also seen the empty tomb.

What was a Jewish-Christian community, a people centered in the Sabbath but now deeply immersed in a Christian community as well, to do with that?

Many of the early Jewish Christians, history tells us, did both. They kept the Sabbath from Friday evening to Saturday evening, as usual, and then met again on Sunday evenings to anticipate that the Jesus who had returned to them out of the grave would soon return to them again.[1]

While there was no formal or uniform liturgical format among the various Christian communities for at least a hundred years after the Crucifixion of Jesus, nonetheless, Christians everywhere came together on Sunday—beginning the very Sunday after the Resurrection—to sing songs and do readings and remember Him in the breaking of the bread (Acts 2:42; Luke 24:35). It was the natural thing to do. After all, so much of what Jesus had done as signs of new life among them, He had done on a Sunday. He rose from the grave on a Sunday. He appeared to the apostles after His death on that Resurrection Sunday and on Sundays after that. He ascended from their midst, according to the Lucan accounts, on a Sunday (Luke 24:1, 13,

51). And, finally, He breathed the Spirit into them and sent them forth as messengers in His name on a Sunday (John 20:19, 22).[2]

Truly, Sunday is the Lord's Day, "the day that the LORD has made" (Ps. 118:24).

But other factors had meaning as well. These factors were pagan, not Jewish or Christian at all.

> Truly, Sunday is the Lord's Day, "the day that the LORD has made" (Ps. 118:24).

In the Greco-Roman world, the days of the week were named after the planets. When the emperor Aurelian in 321 made the first day of the week Sunday, "the venerable day of the Sun," the Lord's Day as we know it today became official in the Christian community. Only recently declared legal in the Roman Empire under the Edict of Milan's doctrine of religious toleration, Christians now found themselves free to engage in public worship. The place of Sunday, or little Easter, in the Christian community, then, became official. And different. Unlike the Jewish Sabbath, with its emphasis on Creation and Exodus, the Christian Sunday became the memorial of Jesus' death and Resurrection, a moment lived in anticipation of His return. Jesus, rather than a Roman sun god, became to the Christian world "the sun of righteousness" (Mal.

4:2), "the light of the world" (John 8:12), "the true light, which enlightens everyone" (John 1:9).

In the conscious choice of Sunday as the focal point of Christianity, the distinction between Sabbath and Sunday became clear.

Sabbath, the sweet day of rest that followed the work of creation, the Jewish world knew, would be the character of the life to come. However much the two have been confused over the years, the Christian Sunday focused instead on the death and Resurrection of Jesus and the awareness that the life to come was already with us—but not yet entirely. The purpose of Sunday, therefore, is not to stop Christians from working in observance of God's rest in the beauty of creation; it is meant to immerse them in reflection on God's place in their lives and their place in the life of the world.

Sunday is, therefore, the original Christian feast day, the axle of liturgical time. It creates the Christian assembly. It immerses us in the good news of Jesus, the unique Son of God, the center of the faith. It emphasizes the place of Jesus in the community after the Resurrection. It strengthens us to endure the darkness of life, to continue our own journeys to the cross, whatever those crosses may be, and to trust that Resurrection is the will of God for us all.

Sunday is not a rest from physical labor; it is the rest of holy leisure, of holy reflection, meant to remind us once again that we have been created to make the world a better place, as Jesus did. It rekindles in us the joy of liberation from the chains of death. It encourages in us the gratitude that comes with having been emancipated from the limitations and seductions of this world. It reminds us week after week of the responsibility of those who, having been freed themselves, must now go on to free others.

It is on Sunday, when we gather to walk with Jesus on the road from Galilee to Jerusalem, that we find ourselves in the Jesus story. We discover that we have been both good Samaritans and lapsed heirs, humble publicans and arrogant debtors, the greedy Dives and the poor Lazarus. We come face-to-face with ourselves in the crowds around Jesus and try again to follow Him more closely, more faithfully, more sincerely.

It is on Sunday when, lost in the singing and reading and breaking of the bread, we discover a bit more about God.

Indeed, Sunday is meant to be a different kind of day. It is on Sunday when, lost in the singing and reading and breaking of the bread, we discover a bit more about who is our God. We see what kind of God this is. Most of all, we discover, often to our chagrin, more about who we are too.

6

HUMAN TIME, LITURGICAL TIME

THE BOOK OF ECCLESIASTES IS CLEAR ABOUT THE nature of time. "There is," the writer tells us, "a time for every purpose under heaven" (Eccl. 3:1 NKJV). For peace and war, for embracing and holding back, for love and hate and planting and reaping, for birthing and dying, for mourning and dancing. For everything. Perhaps nothing so serves to keep the Christian aware of all those dimensions of life than does the progress of liturgical time.

Liturgical time is the arc that affixes the layers of life. It binds heaven and earth into one and the same rhythm. Rather than give ourselves totally to life as we know it here and now, liturgical time raises our sights above the dailiness of life to the essence of life.

The liturgical year, with its great traversal from life to death to life again, carries us from one pole of time to the other with a sense of purpose and progress. It makes us aware of the presence of the kind of time that is not time, that is not our understanding of time, that is beyond time. The liturgical year wraps us in a kind of dual consciousness—of this early life and the life beyond. It reminds us that there is more to us than one kind of life alone, more than one dimension of time, more than one purpose in life.

> *Liturgical time raises our sights above the*
> *dailiness of life to the essence of life.*

Natural time requires us to think of ourselves as moving from energy to decay. This is a life bounded by years of toil, years of diminishment, a movement from more physical life to less physical life. Liturgical time, with its concentration on the spirit, enables us to see ourselves moving from spiritual emptiness to spiritual fulfillment, from less of one dimension of life to more of another deeper, more meaningful kind of life.

Every week of liturgical life brings us closer and closer to the heart of things, farther and farther away from the superficial, from the transient, from what fades and dies, and closer to what enables us to grow even as we may seem most to be declining.

The story is told of a disciple who heard the voice of God calling, "Who is it there?" and the disciple answered, "It is I, Lord." But the voice disappeared.

Years later, the voice called again, and the disciple answered, "It is I, Lord. It is I." And the voice went silent a second time.

Finally, years after, the voice called a third time, "Who is it there?" This time the disciple answered, "It is You, Lord. Only You."

The liturgical year is about putting down our worship of the self and growing more into the One who calls us.

It is in the weekly submersion in the liturgy, in the yearly experience of the life of Jesus with its ebbs and flows, that we become more spiritually mature ourselves. It is watching Jesus deal with those unlike Him that may eventually pry open our closed hearts to foreigners in our own society. It is seeing Jesus deal compassionately with sinners that may save us from the despair of our own weaknesses. It is realizing that Jesus enjoyed life, had friends, loved parties, and welcomed the whole world into the ever-growing circle around Him that saves us from a spirituality that can be more neurotic than it is truly spiritual. Finally, it is in coming to know the Jesus whose life was fine-tuned to the voice of God within him and whose death came out of unremitting commitment to the will of God, whatever the cost, that our own life is shaped and reshaped. Over the years we melt into what we seek.

The liturgical year is, then, a mirror of our own, meant

to both grow us in times of incertitude and sustain us in times of struggle. It is teacher and model, well of hope and sign of triumph when we might otherwise lose our way in the confusion of our own struggles.

Drawn like a magnet, year after year, into the life of Jesus in the Gospels, the triumphs of the feasts, the lessons of the seasons, the cycles of spiritual challenge, and the lives of the great spiritual heroes who have gone the way before us, the Scriptures and its scenes, the questions and answers that lie there begin to sing in my heart. Every year, the images and meanings get clearer and clearer until the classic phrases—like words spoken to Peter, "Do you love me?" (John 21:17) and to the thief, "Today you will be with me in Paradise" (Luke 23:43)—begin to mean more than they meant when I did not know what love was or despaired, in the light of my own self-hatred, of ever knowing the love of God.

The writer of Ecclesiastes was right: there is a time in life for everything. And down deep we know, however secure and invincible, loved and successful we may now feel, other times will surely come. The question is, what will save us from the dregs of life when the wine of life has seemed to disappear? Then, the liturgical year, in one of its endless cycles of remembrance of the past and recognition of its ongoing presence in our own lives, reminds us once again that death is not the end, that rebirth of the spirit is always possible to those who are willing to go down into the life of Jesus one more time, hearts open, souls athirst.

Every year we come to the liturgical cycle of the seasons and find them different because we are different too. We are older, wiser, more experienced. We are also more needy, less sure of ourselves, more greedy for life, and less sure of what it really is. Then, we begin to understand the frustration of the Samaritan woman, the bumbling of the apostles, the dilemma of Joseph, who wants to do what is legal and what is good at the same time. Most of all, we see at work in them, as in us, the gradual awareness of who this Jesus really is and what that means for their lives and ours.

> *Every year we come to the liturgical cycle of the seasons*
> *and find them different because we are different too.*

We discover that life is not a straight line. Life is a coil that bends back on itself over and over again. As a result, in every revolution of it from year to year, we find in ourselves both new depths and greater heights. We come back repeatedly, thanks to the unending rounds of the liturgical year, to the basic truths of the spiritual life that God is, that Jesus is our salvation, that the Spirit is with us, and that we are loved.

Clearly, the liturgical year, relentless in its rhythms and cycles, brings new depth and meaning to the recurrent patterns of our own.

7

THE PLACE OF
WORSHIP IN
HUMAN LIFE

TO BE HUMAN IS TO STRUGGLE BETWEEN TWO EMO-
tional magnets. On the one hand lies the temptation to give
in to a sense of total abjection. After all, humanity is mor-
tal, is limited, is feckless, is a history of disasters. On the
other hand, there hovers in the unbounded awareness of
what it means to be human, the probability of sinking into
unbounded arrogance. Humanity is, after all, also a bundle
of beauty, a reservoir of ability, a possibility unlimited.

The moral question that arises from that dual awareness is clearly an important one, a real one. Just who are
we? Are we, in our humanity, something glorious or are
we, at base, actually nothing much at all? Of the two alter-
natives, neither is really adequate; both are dangerous.

If humanity is nothing more than the decaying top of

a collapsing food chain, then abjection is the only reasonable human response to life. The question of human purpose looms large. The image of an anthill of humanity stumbling through life for no other reason than to die threatens everything humanity has ever managed to create. What is the use of order? Who cares about what we do? Isn't human life nothing more than a large-scale game of "king of the hill," the goal of which is to become king by capturing the hill from someone else? At any cost, perhaps. By whatever means, surely. What else is there to do but to murder, rape, and plunder if murder, rape, and plunder are the essential nature of the human, the order of the day? Then what becomes of ideas like family and honor, truth and compassion?

Aren't humans, too, then, as whole schools of ethnologists say, just one more level of animal life "red in tooth and claw"?[1]

If, on the other hand, humanity is a glorious creature, bright of mind and enlightened of soul, then what limits are necessary? What boundaries are acceptable? And at the same time, how do we explain the neediness under the arrogance? How do we explain blunder after blunder, mistake after mistake, sin after sin? How do we trust ourselves to people who trust themselves too much?

It is a pitiable position, this inherent struggle in us between a sense of hopeless degradation and a posture of terminal arrogance. The psalmist put it clearly and prayed, "What are we that you should care for us?" in one place and "We are little less than the angels" in another (paraphrased). Unsure which is which, we go through life torn between the two. Abjection threatens to turn our weary souls to dust. Arrogance promises to turn our world into nuclear dust and ecological devastation that stems from the human thirst for power and domination.

Only the awareness of a universe whose Creator is outside and above the boundaries of humanity can save us from either the curse of futility or the devastating consequences of self-satisfaction unfulfilled. It is God that humanity needs in order to complete itself. It is knowledge of God that defends us from despair and, at the same time, brings the saving grace of humility that comes with knowing our place in the universe.

It is this awareness of the place of God in life on which the liturgical year turns, bringing us to participate in the life of Jesus in the bringing of the reign of God, giving us the strength it takes to move between the two poles of life with grace, with surety.

The Hebraic story of God's self-revelation to the people of Israel is the ground on which Christian devotion stands. Emmanuel—"God with us"—makes life possible and all our efforts worthwhile. The awareness of a God who moves with us through life is the insight that drives us beyond despair. Here is the God who is indeed above creation but identifies with it at the same time. Here is the God who cares for us.

The Christian story of the death and Resurrection of Jesus, on the other hand, is the call to recognize the resplendency of humanity. This God, in Jesus, has become someone just like us—the One who is "the way" (John 14:6), the One who has shared life with us. This Jesus knows of what we are made and at the same time frees us from ourselves to be more than we are. Here is the God who saves us from the arrogance of worshipping ourselves, and, by having shared in our humanity, makes us glorious at the same time. It is the grounding of faith in the God who makes humanity the stuff of the divine that the Christian community brings to the world.

> *It is the grounding of faith in the God who makes humanity the stuff of the divine that the Christian community brings to the world.*

It is this humility, this consciousness of God in our lives, this truth of who and what we are, this awareness of who and what God is, that can deliver us from ourselves for the sake of the rest of the human race. Without doubt, a worshipping humanity is a healthy humanity.

To know our place in the universe is to recognize that God is God. We are not the masters of the world. We can make no demands on it. All we can do is to try to live our place in it well.

Knowing our limits while we stretch them to their fullest at the same time relieves us of the burden of striving for the perfection we can never reach. More than that, it lifts us to unimaginable heights of surety and trust, of calm and of faith. The God who made us what we are knows what we desire to be and waits with infinite patience while we become what we can. We, on the other hand, know that whatever we need to become all that we can be, this same great and loving God will supply. For all of that, we are thankful. From that gratitude grow love and commitment, faith and trust, wonder and worship.

Worship is the natural overflow of those who, with humble and grateful heart, understand their place in the universe and live in awe of the God who made it so. Worship is the heart of the liturgical year.

8

CALENDARS

WHEN YOU'RE GROWING UP, YOU HAVE FEWER answers to the mysteries of life than the adults around you, so you ask a lot more questions. The problem is that a child asks questions about things most adults normally can't answer, so they learn early to stop asking them. Like, what are black holes? Or, why can't we stop death? Or, where is heaven? Or, where does the sun come from and how did it get there? No wonder children stop asking questions. After all, it makes a kind of good sense to let things that can't be explained go by without being explained. Better no answer at all sometimes than to go on propagating the wrong one. As in, the world is flat.

But childhood questions about the liturgical year are generally simple ones like, when was Jesus born? Why do some people have Christmas one day and other people another one? After all, a birthday is a birthday, isn't it?

Few adults, however, attempt to answer questions that deal with the calculation of something as important, as significant, as the date of Christmas. The liturgical year, it seemed, was simply an arbitrary arrangement of historical dates independent of one another and unrelated in their purpose. The answer to the question of how a date as significant as Christmas could differ from one part of the church to the other had, then, either to be a matter of faith or a matter of error that, therefore, really didn't matter at all.

But the question remains, nevertheless: how can it be possible that different people have different dates for Christmas? We are talking, after all, about the birth of Jesus, no small matter to the credibility of the faith surely. My Greek friends, for instance, have Christmas on one day, and we have another. The Russian Orthodox have even another. How can that be? How can people possibly disagree about such a particular as that? Who of us is right and who is wrong, and what are the implications for the faith if they are right and we aren't?

The truth is that, as simple as the question may seem at first sight, it is far more difficult to answer, even now, than would appear to be the case. And yet, at the same time, the fact that it can't be answered is one of the very things that make the point: the date is simply not important. Christmas is not really about the celebration of a birth date at all. It is about the celebration of a birth. The fact of the date and the fact of the birth are two different things. The calendrical verification of the feast itself is not really that important. In fact, not knowing the actual date of an occurrence, not really caring if we know it or not, actually serves to make the fine distinction between the meaning of the liturgical year and the meaning of the cultural or cultic accretions that are prone to develop in any institution over the ages.

The real answer to the question of the various dates of the liturgical year is that the liturgical year is not, for the most part, about a series of events at all. It is about the import of those defining events. It is about the relationship of those events, one to the other. It is about the real meaning, not the historical dating, of the events which, to this very day, shape our spiritual lives.

> *The liturgical year is not, for the most part, about a series of events at all. It is about the import of those defining events.*

That reality is a lot less unusual in the explication of the great moments in the life of a people, a nation, a religion than it may, at first sight, seem. Actuality is, at best, a memory of something that is greater than the time or place in which it happened. What is important to the understanding of a life-changing moment is that it happened, not necessarily where or when it happened.

Signs all over the eastern United States say, "George Washington slept here." Tour guides in Syria assure people that "St. Paul walked on this street." Pieces of Noah's ark "have been found on this mountain," the brochures say in Turkey. But the fact is that most of the places guaranteed to be genuine artifacts of another age didn't even exist then. At most, the signs indicate that once upon a time the presence of a particular figure was known to have been in this region, or even this area. It does not guarantee geographical precision or historical accuracy. Monte Cassino in Italy, famed Benedictine abbey of the seventh century, for instance, was bombed to the ground in World War II. So is its rebuilt self really Monte Cassino or not? And, in the same way, does it matter seriously to the real history of the United States whether we know the places George Washington stayed as he rose to power?

There are clearly some things, of course, about which knowing the date is essential to the story itself. The date of Napoleon's invasion of Russia, for instance, or the Vietnamese Tet Offensive was germane to the course of these wars. There are other things, however, for which a date has limited or no meaning to the real character of the material with which we're dealing. And, surprisingly enough, Christmas is one of them.

Why don't we know for sure the date of the birth of Jesus? Because it depends on which of that era's calendars we're using to compute it—the solar calendar, the lunar calendar, the Babylonian calendar, the Roman calendar, or the Julian calendar. They weren't uniform then, and they aren't uniform now. In fact, they can't be uniform because they are based on different and distinct methods of calculation. The earth and the moon do not revolve at the same rate of speed. Egypt and Israel did not make up in the same way for time lost during what we call leap years. Later calendars sought to universalize time by agreeing, for practical reasons, as we do now, on devices like date lines and period lengths to make up for the "lost time" incurred by the movement of the spheres.

Another interesting thing about calendars—beyond the fact that they differ depending on the base used to compute them—is that, though calendars tell us what events precede which in any given system, the fact that one thing precedes another does not necessarily make it more important than what follows it. The liturgical year is like that too.

The liturgical year begins with the first Sunday of Advent, and Advent is the four-week preparation period for Christmas. But Christmas is really not the acme of the liturgical year. Christmas simply commemorates, not celebrates, the historical birth of Jesus, whenever that might have been. Because of Christmas, the life of Jesus was possible. Because of Christmas, the Incarnation can be fulfilled at Easter. Because of Christmas, the humanity of Jesus is fact. But the birth of Jesus is not the central meaning of the faith. On the contrary, it is the death and Resurrection of Jesus that are the core of Christianity.

> *The birth of Jesus is not the central meaning of the faith. On the contrary, it is the death and Resurrection of Jesus that are the core of Christianity.*

The liturgical year is, then, actually about Easter. It is about the Crucifixion and the Resurrection of Jesus, about the cross and the empty tomb, about the intersection of the life of Jesus with the rest of humankind, with us and our lives, with us and our death. The historicity of Christmas simply attests to the fact that Jesus was human, did live, and did die. Easter is much more than that. Easter is about the very center of the faith, about the vision of life it instills in us, the meaning of faith it gives us, the redemption of soul it offers us. Every event in the liturgical year points to that reality. Nothing else in the Christian culture so completely explains all other things Christian as well as Easter does.

It's not surprising then that the church never spent much time worrying about the exact date of the birth of Jesus. In an era of multiple calendars, many groups counted the turning of nights and days in different ways, according to the custom of the area. Even the very definition of *day* differed from one group to another. The Jewish day, for instance, began and ended at sunset in conformity with a lunar calendar. Greeks, at the same time, measured days from dawn to dawn. And the Romans, like us, who reckoned time by the sun, counted their days from midnight to midnight. Determining months with any kind of unanimity under such disparate systems was clearly impossible. To determine what happened when in such ancient cultures is hardly possible and never uniform. Calendrical conformity was a lost art for centuries and, in some systems, does not exist yet.

In the Western world, it took six centuries to even begin to define a common calendar throughout the church. Centralization in the church was at best loose and local. Calendars were more a mathematical or astrological exercise than an exact science.

At the time of the life of Jesus, there were at least five major calendars in use in the area: the lunar calendar of the Jewish community, the solar calendar of the Greeks, a Julian calendar, a Roman calendar, and a Byzantine calendar, among others. In fact, to this very day, the Armenian church has no Christmas feast, with the exception of the Armenian churches in union with Rome.[1]

The message is clear: Christmas is not about marking

the actual birth date of Jesus. It is about the Incarnation of the One who became like us in all things but sin (Heb. 4:15) and who humbled Himself "to the point of death—even death on a cross" (Phil. 2:8). Christmas is a pinnacle feast, yes, but it is not the beginning of the liturgical year. It is a memorial, a remembrance, of the birth of Jesus, not really a celebration of the day itself. We remember that because the Jesus of history was born, the Resurrection of the Christ of faith could happen.

Christmas, then, like all the other feasts of the liturgical year, is really about Easter. It is about turning our faces, with the historical Jesus, toward the Jerusalem of our own life, knowing that there at the cross and the tomb of Jesus are our strength and our hope, our beginning and our end, both now and forever.

> *Christmas, then, like all the other feasts of the liturgical year, is really about Easter.*

With that certainty in mind, then, the Christian moves from one dimension of the liturgical year to the next, making the journey of soul from Nazareth to Bethlehem to Jerusalem with the Jesus who began in obscurity and ended in glory, who came to bring the reign of God and died for its coming, who was born in a stable and rose from a tomb. This is the Jesus who came to show us all how to free ourselves from the chains of self in order to live with God. Even here. Even now.

It is because of this we celebrate Christmas. With that consciousness of the coming of new life, therefore, we begin the liturgical year with Advent, the season of anticipation, the beginning of readiness.

9

ADVENT: THE HUMAN EXPERIENCE OF WAITING

WHEN ALL THE FEASTS HAVE BEEN CELEBRATED AND all the prayers are said and done, the strength and power of the liturgical year does not lie in its cataloging of feast days and seasons, as important as these are. Nor does it lie in its rubrics and rituals. The real power of the liturgical year is its spiritual capacity to touch and plumb the depths of the human experience, to stir the human heart. By walking the way of the life of Jesus, by moving into the experience of Jesus, we discover the meaning of our own experiences, the undercurrent of our own emotions, the struggle it takes to go on walking the way.

By taking us into the depth of what it means to be a human on the way to God—to suffer and to wonder, to know abandonment and false support, to believe and to doubt—the liturgical year breaks us open to the divine. It gives us the energy to become the fullness of ourselves. It makes the next step possible. It calms us as we stumble from one to the other. It leads us beyond our present selves to the self that lies in wait for God.

> *By taking us into the depth of what it means to be a human on the way to God . . . the liturgical year breaks us open to the divine.*

The liturgical year does not begin at the heart of the Christian enterprise. It does not immediately plunge us into the chaos of the Crucifixion or the giddy confusion of the Resurrection. Instead, the year opens with Advent, the season that teaches us to wait for what is beyond the obvious. It trains us to see what is behind the apparent. Advent makes us look for God in all those places we have, until now, ignored.

A friend recently gave me a textile wall-hanging from Peru that makes clear that the process of finding God in the small things of life is as profound as it is simple. A pastoral scene of palm trees and rural lean-tos has been hand-stitched by peasant women, quilt-style, across the top of a felt banner. Under it is a calendar of thirty small pockets, each of them filled with something we can't see. Every day until Christmas, we are invited to find the part of the scene that has been pocketed for that day and attach it to the scene above, one piece of handwoven cloth adhering to the other as we go.

Some of the pieces are of benign and beautiful things; some are not. There are bumble bees and angels, wild animals and dry straw, a branch-laden peasant man and a weary-looking woman. But there at the end of the days, as common as all the rest of the items in the scene, is the manger, the sign of the One who knows what life is like for us, who has mixed His own with ours. Now, we can see, all our expectations have been worth it.

Advent is about learning to wait. It is about not having to know exactly what is coming tomorrow, only that whatever it is, it is of the essence of sanctification for us. Every piece of it, some hard, some uplifting, is sign of the work of God alive in us. We are becoming as we go. We learn in Advent to stay in the present, knowing that only the present well lived can possibly lead us to the fullness of life.

Life is not meant to be escaped, we learn, as the liturgical year moves from season to season, from feast to feast. It is meant to be penetrated, to be plumbed to its depths, to be tasted and savored and bring us to realize that the God who created us is with us yet. Life, we come eventually to know, is an exercise in transformation, the mechanics of which take a lifetime of practice, of patience, of slow, slow growth.

Clearly, then, learning to wait is an essential dimension of spiritual development. It has its own values, bringing its own character to the process of becoming spiritually mature.

Waiting hones our insights. It gives us the time and space, the perspective and patience that enable us to discriminate between the good, the better, and the best. It is so simple to go through life blind to the wealth of its parts, swallowing life whole, oblivious to its punctuation points. Then we fail to call ourselves to the small, daily demands of compassion or choice, trust or effort. If we do not learn to wait, we can allow ourselves to assume that one thing really is as good for us as another. Then we forget that life is about more than this life. We race over the top of it, satiating ourselves with the obvious, unmindful of its depths. We become stale of soul. We fail to grow spiritually.

It is waiting that attunes us to the invisible in a highly material world. In contemporary society, what counts is what we can get and what we have. Instead of listening for the voice of God in the winds of change around us, we can come to hear only our own.

The function of Advent is to remind us what we're waiting for as we go through life too busy with things that do not matter to remember the things that do. When year after year we hear the same scriptures and the same hymns of longing for the life to come, of which this one is only its shadow, it becomes impossible to forget the refrains of the soul.

Advent relieves us of our commitment to the frenetic in a fast-paced world. It slows us down. It makes us think.

It makes us look beyond today to the "great tomorrow" of life. Without Advent, moved only by the race to nowhere that exhausts the world around us, we could be so frantic with trying to consume and control this life that we fail to develop within ourselves a taste for the spirit that does not die and will not slip through our fingers like melted snow.

It is while waiting for the coming of the reign of God, Advent after Advent, that we come to realize that its coming depends on us. What we do will either hasten or slow, sharpen or dim our own commitment to do our part to bring it.

> *It is while waiting for the coming of the reign of God, Advent after Advent, that we come to realize that its coming depends on us.*

Waiting—that cold, dry period of life when nothing seems to be enough and something else beckons within us— is the grace that Advent comes to bring. It stands before us, within us, pointing to the star for which the wise ones from the East are only icons of ourselves.

We all want something more. Advent asks the question, what is it for which you are spending your life? What is the star you are following now? And where is that star in its present radiance in your life leading you? Is it a place that is really comprehensive enough to equal the breadth of the human soul?

10

THE VOICE
OF ADVENT

WHEN THE FIRST SMALL FLAME OF THE ADVENT wreath lights the monastery chapel and the soft, clear voices of those who have sung the chants and haunting melodies all their lives open the first of the Advent vigils, there is no doubt that we have begun a moment out of time. It is the beginning of the liturgical year. Christmas is four weeks away. We are at the moment in which a new cycle of old ideas will be stirred up again within us. We are beginning a spiritual crossing on dark waters led only by an ancient sailing chart marked by a star. Here in the dark we will begin the search for light in the soul.

Advent is not the oldest season in the church. Easter, the Pasch or Passover, is far older, by at least two hundred years. Advent did not begin in Rome. In fact, the earliest mention of a period of preparation for Christmas didn't exist until 490 in Gaul, what is now modern France.[1]

We are not here in this dark chapel tonight, then, because Christmas is the high point of every church year, and Advent its most profound season. The church year does not start here because Christmas is coming. The church year starts here to remind us why Jesus was born in the first place. Most of all, it starts here to call us to determine why we ourselves are here at all.

Advent, from the Latin, means "coming." But Advent is not about one coming; it is about three comings. The great spiritual question the season poses for each of us is, which coming are you and I waiting for now? At this moment of our lives, at this present stage of our spiritual development, what we're waiting for surely determines how we will wait for it.

> *The great spiritual question the season poses for each of us is, which "coming" are you and I waiting for now?*

Each of the three comings of Advent is very different. The first coming is the remembrance of the birth of Jesus of Nazareth in the flesh, based on the infancy narratives in the Gospels that give its historical context. But if our expectation of Christmas remains at this level, the birthday of the "baby Jesus" becomes at best a pastoral attempt to

make Jesus real. This Jesus is a child's Jesus that, too often—
if our definition of Christmas is simply a child's story about
the birth of a child—will remain just that. It is a simple,
soothing story that makes few, if any, demands on the soul.

This coming too often leaves us, whatever our age, at the
stage of spiritual childhood. The baby Jesus captivates our
hearts, true. But the birth date of this child is not one of the
great mysteries of the faith. As Augustine pointed out, "The
day of the Lord's birth does not possess a sacramental character. It is only a recalling of the fact that he was born."[2]

The next coming to which Advent calls our attention
is a coming greater than the simple fact of human birth.
This is the coming of the presence of God recognized
among us now in the Scripture, in the Eucharist, in the
community itself. This coming makes Jesus present in our
own lives, eternally enlivening, eternally with us.

The final coming to which Advent points us is the
Second Coming, the Parousia. It is this coming that whets
the desire of the adult soul. At the end of time, Jesus has
promised and the Christian believes that the Son will return
in glory. Then the reign of God for which we strive with
every breath will come in all its fullness. This is the coming
for which we wait. This is the fullness for which we long. This
is what we really mean when the choir sings into the dark,
"Maranatha." "Come, Lord Jesus, come" is one rendering
of the word. But taken from the Greek, as *maran atha*—two

words—"The Lord *has* come" is another equally acceptable translation.[3] Then the comings—past, present, and future— all live together in one long sigh of the soul.

Over the centuries and out of many traditions, Advent as we know it now—a four-week period of concentrated waiting—has emerged to center us in these multiple layers of awareness, in these many levels of faith, in these varied plies of spiritual maturity. We grow from one to the other, realizing as we do, that life is about more than the past, even about more than the present, and certainly, in the end, about the fullness of a future that is far longer than even our own.

Advent is a period of preparation for Christmas but, unlike Lent, it is not a period of penance. It is a period that focuses us on joy. We prepare ourselves to understand the full adult meaning of the feast. We come to realize more each year how great are our blessings, how beautiful is a life lived in concert with the Jesus who came to show us the way. We learn the joy of anticipation, the joy of delighting in a sense of the presence of God all around us, the joy of looking for the second coming of Christ, the joy of living in the surety of even more life in the future.

Advent unlike Lent, it is not a period of penance.
It is a period that focuses us on joy.

The voice of Advent in our ears is loud and clear year after year. Its three-year cycle of Scripture winds over and around us, reminding us, assuring us, prodding us to bear Christ in our own lives. Every week of the four-week period, one or other of the three-year round of readings is a clear call to the multiple meanings of Advent.

The first week of Advent reminds us of the Old Testament call for the Messiah to usher in the kingdom of peace and the New Testament call to watch and wait for the Second Coming whose "day is at hand" (Rom. 13:12 NKJV).

The second week of Advent calls us with John the Baptist to repent, to be pure and blameless so that our own exile, like the exile of the chosen people, can be ended when we, too, grow to full spiritual stature.

The third week of Advent, Gaudete Sunday, the week to rejoice because the Lord is near, leaves us with two great gospel images. The first focuses us on Jesus' answer to John's question, "Are you the one who is to come, or are we to wait for another?" (Matt. 11:3). And the response comes back, "Go and tell John what you hear and see: the blind receive their sight, the lame walk, the lepers are cleansed, the deaf hear, the dead are raised, and the poor have good news brought to them" (Matt. 11: 4–5). This Jesus, we learn if we are really looking for Him, is to be found with the poor and the needy, the outcast and the oppressed.

The second image is of John reminding us that we must "prepare the way of the Lord" (Mark 1:3). We must do more than simply go through the Advent calendar; we must develop in us an Advent heart.

> *We must do more than simply go through the*
> *Advent calendar; we must develop in us an Advent heart.*

The third week of the cycle, John lays out the lifestyle of those who will see the Second Coming: "Whoever has two coats must share with anyone who has none; and whoever has food must do likewise" (Luke 3:11). The point is clear: it is not simply a matter of waiting and rejoicing in what Advent promises us. It is about learning how to live while we wait.

Finally, the readings for the fourth week of Advent remind us of Joseph's doubts about the pregnant Mary, about Mary's struggle to understand the unacceptable, about Elizabeth's faith in the unpredictable will of God. Now we understand: we, too, must face the doubts that plague our own faith and say once more with Mary, "I will"—whatever that means, wherever that leads. The great endeavor of the spiritual life, the great challenge to the faith, the great exertion of the soul, begins here, then, at the very moment the joy is greatest and the awareness of God with us is most palpable. We begin now, in Advent, whether we realize it or not, to prepare for Easter—because Easter is the reason Christmas is important.

The journey that begins on the first Sunday of Advent at the beginning of this new liturgical year will not end till we, too, reach the cross and the empty tomb, remember the Ascension and the going from us, recall Pentecost and the outpouring of the Advocate, and call to mind again the Second Coming at the end of time. Then, perhaps, we will be centered on our own final step into the arms of God when this time ends.

It is an awesome overview of the territory ahead of us of which the choir begins to sing that first night in the dark chapel. But as the year goes by, the light gets brighter and brighter.

11

JOY: THE ESSENCE
OF IT ALL

An old adage teaches, "Joy is not in things; it is in us." Learning what it is that makes us happy is the task of a lifetime. And, oh, we stumble along doing it. We try it all. And fail at most.

We scatter ourselves looking for pleasure—going here, tasting this, wanting those, getting that. But pleasure is fleeting and can only be maintained for as long as we can physically tolerate what it takes to get it. Once "pleasured," it is necessary, then, to ratchet up the ante, to do more of what satisfied us in the first place. So we drink more. Or we gamble more and so lose more. Or we eat more till eating itself is our problem. Or we play more. Or run more. Or buy more. Until all the joy of it runs out. Then pleasure doesn't work anymore. We simply have no capacity for tickling left in us. We jade ourselves trying.

We exhaust ourselves looking for wealth. But the harder we work, the more money we make, the less there is left to do with it. There are only so many things we can buy until we have bought the best over and over again. There are only so many things we can use and still enjoy using them. In the end, then, money is really useless. It can fly us into the Amazon, but it cannot give us the joy of smelling the rain forest unless we are willing to give up the plane and stay awhile. Before long, it becomes clear: as the Kenyans say, "Those who have cattle have care." The palling pursuit of wealth, we learn too late, simply diminishes the deep-down joy of having it. It is convenient, yes, but fulfilling, no.

Finally, we diminish ourselves by basking in self-exultation. The more self-centered we become, the less we have to make us happy. Despite our raging internal need to get all the attention in the room, all the light on the stage, all the applause in the crowd, we find ourselves more and more isolated, less and less filled up by it. We have no one now to turn to for the love we want and cannot find. We have made ourselves the love of our lives and found little to adore at the altar of our egos. We have made ourselves our own gods and have forgotten God in the process.

The joy and happiness we sought has not come from spending life in an orgy of self-love, self-satisfaction, and self-aggrandizement. Joy, the deep-down awareness of what it means to live well, to live productively, to live righteously, is made out of self-giving, simplicity, and other-centeredness. Ironically enough, in a world that finds religion dour, accuses it of being nothing but a list of dos and don'ts designed to limit our options and trammel our dreams, it is precisely the journey to joy that the liturgical year is all about.

The truth is that the Christmas season, the very entrée to the liturgical year, is unabashed about the purpose of the Christian life. "I am bringing you good news of great joy," the angel says to the shepherds on the hillside outside of Bethlehem about the birth of a baby in a stable there (Luke 2:10). Good news of great joy, we learn at the beginning of the liturgical year, is what searching for the baby is all about. It's how and where we're searching that matters.

"Happiness is a choice that requires effort at times," the Greek playwright Aeschylus wrote. But that's wrong. Happiness does not require choice some of the time. Happiness requires choice all the time. It requires learning to choose between what is real and what is fleeting, what is worthless and what is worthwhile. But that does not make the effort either impossible or unacceptable. It simply requires discrimination.

It is discrimination, the ability to choose between one good in life over another, that the liturgical year parades before our eyes over and over again, year after year, until we finally develop enough maturity of soul to tell what lasts from what pales, to discern what's worth having from what isn't, to know what happiness is rather than what satiety is.

Advent and the Christmas season show us life in its essence. In it, we are brought face-to-face with life stripped down and effulgent at the same time, simple and radiant at once. Here in the Child is promise and meaning, purpose and potential. "I'm bringing you," the angel says, "good news of great joy for all the people: to you is born this day . . . a Savior, who is the Messiah, the Lord" (Luke 2:10–11).

The question with which the liturgical year confronts us at the beginning of the season, then, is a direct one: what does the life of Jesus now mean to us? How is this life affecting our own? Are we ourselves living both the promise and the potential?

> *The question with which the liturgical year confronts us is a direct one: what does the life of Jesus now mean to us?*

Meaning, we discover, has nothing to do with what is outside of us. It has to do with what we have come to see with our souls. It has to do with the vision that is within us rather than with the things we are heaping up around us as indicators of our success, our power, our status. Joy is not about what happens to us, the manger indicates. It is the meaning we give to what we do that determines the nature, the quality of the lives we live.

Joy is not about self-centeredness, the manger insists. "I seek to do not my own will but the will of him who sent me" the Scriptures remind us of this Child (John 5:30). No doubt about it: happiness is not about self-satisfaction; it is about the joy that comes with a sense of purpose. It is not about self-aggrandizement; it is about living our lives immersed in the will of God. At the end of the day, life and joy, success and happiness are about otherness.

"The essential of happiness," Allan K. Chalmers wrote, "is having something to do, something to love and something to hope for."[1] At the very outset of the liturgical year, the church presents a model of them all: a Child who lives only to do the will of God, who opens His arms to love the entire world, who lives in hope of the coming of the reign of God by giving His life to bring it. At the very outset of the year, we are given the model of how to be happy.

> *At the very outset of the year, we are given the model of how to be happy.*

The purpose of the liturgical year, Advent is clear, is not to confine the human being to a life of neurotic abnegation and miserable self-denial for its own sake. It is a year meant to show us in flesh and blood what it really takes to be happy. If that does not happen for us, it is only because we have yet to understand what we're seeing. We have yet to get the message that, indeed, joy is not in things; it is in us.

If, focused on the Christ Child at the very beginning of the liturgical year, we do not have the spiritual vision to see meaning there and to develop it within ourselves, there is nothing else on earth that will ever be able to supply it for us.

12

CHRISTMAS:
THE COMING
OF THE LIGHT

DESPITE ALL THE ATTEMPTS TO MAKE CALENDARS square with the event, no one is really sure what date Jesus was born. The origin of the feast of Christmas, in fact, is an obscure one entirely. Why it started, exactly where it started, or who started it is completely unclear. But what is not obscure is that, for centuries, there have been two totally distinct Christmas celebrations. And there still are.

One Christmas celebration, started in the West, is December 25. The second Christmas celebration, begun in the East, is January 6. Both of them have been ab-sorbed into the liturgical calendar of the other, but for different reasons and in different ways. The theories about the beginnings of these feasts give new insight into both.

The first of the theories involves the importance of astronomy and astrology to the period. Solstices and equinoxes that came during the last days of the last month of every quarter of the year—March, June, September, and December—signaled the turn of the seasons. Solstices occur either of two times of the year when the sun is at its greatest distance from the celestial equator. The summer solstice in the Northern Hemisphere occurs about June 21, the longest day of the year, when the sun is at its highest point from the earth. The winter solstice occurs about December 21, the shortest day of the year.

Equinoxes, those times when day and night are of equal length, also occur twice a year. In the north, the spring equinox occurs about March 21, the autumn equinox about September 22.

In ancient societies, both occasions gave rise to liturgical as well as to calendrical significance. Solstices and equinoxes are the astrological signals of the change of seasons. As a result, fertility festivals, with their rites of spring and the coming of new light in the depth of winter, were moments of great significance in an agricultural society. What greater months than those, March and December, solstice and equinox, to celebrate a divine breakthrough into the realm of humanity?

A second theory put forward to explain the two separate Christmas celebrations involves the principle of symmetry, the exact correspondence of one date to another. According to the conventional wisdom of the time, greatness was signaled by the symmetry of a person's date of birth and date of death. Great personages, it was assumed, were born and died on the same date. From that perspective, the date of Jesus' birth could be determined by the date of his death, and that could be calculated from the date of the Jewish Passover, of course. So, at least according to some, Jesus' death and conception would have been March 25. According to the principle of symmetry, then, the birth of Jesus would have been exactly nine months later on the same date, December 25.[1]

In the East, where the Julian calendar and its system of astrological calculations are still the norm, the Pasch, Easter, is celebrated on April 6. The birth of Jesus, according to these symmetrical reckonings, would then be January 6.

To this day, as a result, the West celebrates Christmas on December 25. The East celebrates Christmas on January 6, both dates having been arrived at by virtue of the principle of symmetry but according to a different method of calculating time.

Christmas in the West began to be celebrated in Rome in 336 and once begun, spread rapidly. But that's a good deal later, for instance, than it was already being celebrated in Spain and Gaul, Switzerland and Belgium, which signals, of course, that the universal celebration of Christmas in the West took centuries to develop.

The third theory concerning the different computations of Christmas is that both Christmas in the West and Epiphany in the East were the Christian answer to pagan feasts—the feast of the sun in the West and, conversely, the winter solstice in the East.

Whichever of the theories might someday be discovered as the origin of either feast, the point is clear: just as the death of Jesus happened at a significant moment, so did His natural birthday signal a world-changing event. With the issuance of the Edict of Milan in 313, Christians could finally worship freely rather than worship the Roman god Sol Invictus, the "invincible sun," on December 25. Christians argued, therefore, that December 25 was really the feast of the "Son of Justice," the true Light who had come to inaugurate the reign of God, to save the world, to change the very notions of life as it had been known until that time. And so, Christmas was officially inaugurated in the West.

Just as the death of Jesus happened at a significant moment, so did His natural birthday signal a world-changing event.

In the East, on the other hand, where the birth of the god Aion was celebrated in Alexandria as part of that culture's recognition of the life-giving winter solstice, January 6 became the Christian feast of the manifestation of Jesus to the world as the Son of God. January 6 was not, therefore, in its earliest days celebrated as the historical birthday of Jesus in the Eastern church. It was instead the celebration of His baptism, His spiritual birthing, when the Son of Man was manifested as the Son of God as well (Mark 1:11).

Whichever of the explanations for the feast gives actual foundation for the dating of the Incarnation, in the end they all come together around the celebration of life, of God's greatness, and of the manifestation of divinity in our midst.

It is this consciousness of the gift of life, of God's greatness and the sense of the divine in our midst, that brings depth to our own life. It is those things that make the celebration of Christmas more than a mere commemoration of an historical birth date. We do not come to Christmas to pretend that the baby Jesus is born again this day. Nor do we pretend that on this day the baby Jesus is born in some mystical way in us. We come to Christmas looking for the signs of Jesus' presence manifested in our own life and age, in us and in the world around us.

On Christmas and Epiphany, in both Eastern and Western celebrations of the birth of Jesus, we are brought to see Jesus incarnated again before our very eyes. When we are tempted to think of the Incarnation as nothing more than the physical birth of Jesus, we are stretched by the Eastern church to see beyond the obvious. Though the Eastern church does not dwell on the birth of Jesus in the flesh, the theology of the East is very clear about His many manifestations of the divine in life. Between the two traditions of Christmas and Epiphany, four strong images emerge of the ongoing presence and power of Jesus in the world to this day. As a result, Christmas and Epiphany can be seen as two aspects of the one feast of Christmas rather than as two distinctly different feasts.

> *Christmas and Epiphany can be seen as two aspects of the one feast of Christmas rather than as two distinctly different feasts.*

First, while the West concentrates on Jesus' manifestation in the flesh, the East celebrates the baptism of Jesus, His manifestation to us as the Son of God. In a period wrestling with the Arian contention that Jesus was human, yes, but not divine, the East reminds us of the scripture "This is My beloved Son, in whom I am well pleased" (Matt. 17:5 NKJV). There is no doubt, the Eastern church shows us, that after the baptism of Jesus, we come to know clearly whose Child this Jesus is. When we are tempted to wonder, like the people of the first three centuries of the church, whether Jesus was simply human, rather than divine as well, the Eastern emphasis on the baptism of Jesus in the Jordan makes the matter crystal clear. This feast is not about the celebration of "the baby Jesus," but it is about the birthing of Jesus of Nazareth as the Son of God.

Second, both feasts underscore and celebrate the manifestation of Jesus to the world through the Magi. The whole world pays homage to the Lord of all in this feast. Jesus is not some kind of merely Christian icon. He is not just another kind of Jewish prophet. This is the One for whom the whole human race waits, whose star we all follow.

Third, Jesus makes manifest His divine power over the things of earth by the inclusion of the changing of the water into wine at the wedding feast of Cana in the liturgical readings.

Finally, in the West, Jesus' coming in the flesh, His being just like us, His growing in age and grace, as we must too, becomes the focus of the feast. Here, Incarnation itself—the humanity of Jesus—is accented. Jesus is the one who is just like us, who shares our lives from beginning to end, who understands us because He is one of us.

Between them, then, the two churches of East and

West celebrate four manifestations of Christ in Christmas: as heavenly Son of God, as King of the nations, as Lord of creation, as human child. Clearly, understanding the meaning behind the celebration of the alternate feast of Christmas/Epiphany provides even deeper understanding of our own at the same time.

This is what the liturgical year focuses us on at the beginning of the year: the clear manifestation of the One we follow through this rehearsal of the life of Jesus year after year. The feast of Christmas/Epiphany attests to the entire arc of Christology. This one is both the God who reaches down to us and the human who raises us up to God.

Christmas is not about a baby, not about sentimental piety, not about Christian fantasy. Christmas is a very adult feast. It stretches us far beyond a manger in Bethlehem. It brings us to recognize who it is that we, like the people of Jesus' own time, will, in everything we do in life this year, either accept or reject.

Jesus is, indeed, the fullness of Advent's "O Antiphons," those piercing prophetic revelations of Isaiah telling us exactly who this is who has come, who is with us now, who is yet to come again. He is Wisdom, Adonai, Flower of Jesse's stem, Key of David, Radiant Dawn, God of all the earth, Emmanuel—God with us.

13

THE CHRISTMAS SEASON: STARS TO STEER BY

THANKSGIVING DINNER IS BARELY CLEARED AWAY NOW before the great secular feast of this age—Christmas shopping, our civic adoration at the shrine of the local economy—begins in blaring frenzy. In the West, at least, it has become a time of frenetic buying, fairy-tale delights, commercial excess, and child-centered fantasy. Santa Claus becomes the "reason for the season" even in Christian homes, and "Merry Christmas" has become "Happy Holidays."

The Christmas season has morphed into the secularization of the salvation of the soul. It has become the secular Advent. We shop and wrap and carry and, in a single moment, rip open packages and cart the torn boxes and ribbons and paper away to wait for the same time next year.

But not for the Christian. For the Christian, the Christmas season is a great deal more than that.

To the Christian steeped in the spirituality of the liturgical year, Christmas is not a single event. It is an entire season of feasts, from December 25 to the Sunday after Epiphany in mid-January. Each of them is designed to take us deeper and deeper into commitment, into understanding, into faith—and most of all, perhaps, into hope. It is a season that puts a glow on the soul. These are feasts that take us into the mystical insights that characterized the First Coming of Jesus and are at least as important to our own faith in the Second Coming of Jesus. Suddenly, in the outpost of Jerusalem, in an empire given to tax collecting and riot control, in a Hebrew community oppressed by a foreign power but nourished by ancient prophecies of hope and liberation, little by little there stirred the awareness among many that somehow the foundations of heaven and earth had been shaken. The world had changed. The pregnancy of human hope and the conviction of divine possibility were in the air.

It's to the three aspects of Christmas itself—the Vigil Mass, Midnight Mass, and the Mass at Dawn—that we are drawn. But Christmas Day is not the whole of the Christmas season. The full scope of Christmas is only experienced in the feasts of the holy family, Mary the mother of God, the Epiphany, and the baptism of Jesus. It is to these other layers of the birth of Jesus that the Christmas season points us. It is not simply the birth of the Child that the season celebrates; it is the awareness of the ongoing work of God within Him, the foundation of our own hope for liberation that marks our lives and lifts our hearts. We are not left wondering, with John the Baptist, whether this is the "one who is to come" (Luke 7:20). We can watch His growth into God, more and more, every step of the way.

Each of the feasts of Christmastide is another star on the horizon of the soul, confirming what our hearts already know: God is with us. The Radiant Dawn has swallowed up the darkness. It is, indeed, the Season of Light.

> *Each of the feasts of Christmastide is another star on the horizon of the soul, confirming what our hearts already know: God is with us.*

But light is more elusive than we like to remember. When the ancients observed the winter solstice, it was with thousands of years of fear that once gone, the light might not come back. It might not, this time, return to warm the earth or grow the seeds or prod the harvests upon which they depended for life. The great ancient monuments—Stonehenge in England, or New Grange, even older, in Ireland—were built to function in the midst of wet, cold, black winter, when darkness was its deepest, its longest, its cruelest. Then the light was tenuous. Then even the days were gray. The monuments were built to catch the first gleam of light after the longest night in the year. When the days were darkest, then the light came. But you couldn't be sure it would. You had to be patient, be hopeful, be strong. It was the return of the light you were celebrating. It was the return of the light that gave reason for hope in another year.

For the chosen people, too, at the time of the birth of Jesus, this was a world in darkness.

By the time Emperor Aurelian first worshipped the Sol Invictus, the "invincible sun" in 274—and then, in 321, declared the day an official "day of rest,"[1] the whole world knew what, in this age, we might be more inclined to take for granted. They knew the meaning of light, the impact of its presence, the fact that we cannot live without it. And the Christians of the empire knew that the light of the soul far transcended the light of the sun.

This small Christian community at the heart of the empire a few hundred years later knew that, for them, the Light that was Jesus had conquered the darkness that had threatened to obliterate them totally.

Now it was for them to live in this light, to fear no darkness ever again, to understand that "the people who walked in darkness" had, indeed, "seen a great light" (Isa. 9:2). These were, after all, the people of the cross and the tomb as well as of the light. They knew, as did no other, that the two events were really one. No manger, no cross. No cross, no empty tomb. It was all of a piece.

In ancient times, the church thought of Christmas as the Passover of Jesus from heaven to earth because of which the Great Pasch, the Passover of Jesus from earth to heaven, was really possible.

Now it was for them to make the Light known, to bring it to others, to bask in its certainty, however dark the nights ahead.

> *Christmas is meant to take us to the level of spiritual maturity where we are capable of seeing in a manger the meaning of an empty tomb.*

The Christmas season, if we see it as a whole rather than as an isolated event (and, in our age, a totally distorted and even misleading conception of the feast) can ignite the spark that will lead us through the darkness of our own lives every day of the year. It is the light of Christmas within us that will take us, if we have the insight to cling to it, beyond a fairy-tale rendering of the great truths of the faith to an understanding of what all the dark days of life are about.

Christmas is not meant to leave us with nothing more than a child's perception of what it means to see a baby in a manger scene. It is meant to take us to the level of spiritual maturity where we are capable of seeing in a manger the meaning of an empty tomb. It is meant to enable us to see through the dark days of life to the stars beyond them.

14

CHRISTMASTIDE: THE FULLNESS OF THE TIME

THERE'S A POPULAR FOLK TALE ABOUT THREE BLIND men who walk around an elephant to determine what kind of beast this animal might be. One takes hold of the elephant's tail and says, "This creature is very like a rope." The second happens to take hold of its tusk and says, "This creature is very like a spear." And the third, patting the wide, hard side of the animal, says, "This creature is surely a wall." Obviously, if any one of them had all three insights at once, these men would have understood a great deal more about elephants than any one of them could possibly know alone.

Liturgical spirituality is a bit like that as well. Each season has a great consuming centerpiece on which we concentrate—Christmas Day or the Resurrection—but it is being willing to walk thoughtfully through all the other parts of each particular cycle that gives us the fuller, truer picture of exactly what the feast itself is all about.

The Christmas season, or Christmastide, is not about one feast day. It is a series of feasts that embed us in a kind of refracted glory, the underpinnings, the other pieces of the mosaic that complete the feast itself.

The feasts of a season create a heightened awareness in us of what the season's major feast is about. They help us to understand the feast from multiple perspectives and various layers of meaning. Together they create a mosaic that fleshes out for us the fullest meaning of the feast. They give us a way of looking at our own world differently because through them we come to see Jesus differently. They provide the hope because of which we can move in the dark parts of the spiritual life with both confidence and conviction.

Christmas—the light that shone upon a manger—was also, the ancients knew, the light that led them on beyond it as well. If God is truly with us, has been manifested among us, companions us as we go, knows our pains and our hopes, then life is not a dark forest from which there is no exit. It is a darkness, however dark, that is always overcome by light.

But how would they know that? How do we know that? We know that because surrounding the feast of Christmas are the feasts that open up to us the real nature of this Child whom, with the shepherds, we have come to realize lives with us, in us, as much today as yesterday. These minor feasts of Christmastide give us a great deal more than a manger. They give us, as adults, models to live by if we, too, are to be steeped in Jesus and full of new life.

> *These minor feasts of Christmastide give us models to live by if we, too, are to be steeped in Jesus and full of new life.*

THE FEAST OF THE HOLY FAMILY

The Feast of the Holy Family depicts Jesus in a home where He grows in wisdom, age, and grace (Luke 2:52). It is a model of what we want for the children of our time. It is a model of the kind of love and care that encourages children to grow up to be on their own but guides them as they do.

This feast causes us to pause and look at our own families, both the ones we grew up in and the ones we're now developing ourselves. It raises questions in us about the harmony of the home we're in now—and what part we play in both its peace and its disturbance. We are brought to wonder what wisdom, maturity, and virtue the children of our time are able to see in us that will transfer itself to them. We must ask ourselves if we are learning from one another, caring for one another, becoming more spiritual together as we go. And if not, why not? And what do we intend to do about it, as Jesus did, for the sake of the rest of the world?

THE OCTAVE OF CHRISTMAS:
THE FEAST OF MARY THE MOTHER OF GOD

Very few feasts have an octave, an eight-day commemoration of the feast, meant to give even more significance to the dignity and importance of the major celebration itself. Like incense, an octave is the sweet memory, eight days later, of what has gone before. It is the aura of a feast, so important, so impacting, that the power of its presence in the human soul lingers far after the feast itself. If nothing else, it is an octave that says to the deepest part of us, *Don't overlook what you have just seen. Think again. Think about it always.*

In that same way, this feast adds another layer to Christmas. The Octave of Christmas, January 1, while we are still very much aware of the birth of Jesus, confronts us with the Solemnity of Mary, Mother of God. But this feast is not the church's answer to the annual Mother's Day so common in the secular world; this feast is a statement about both Mary and Jesus. She is human, we know, and therefore so is He. This Jesus is no Greek god, no being from another planet, no fairy-tale divine. This Child, born of Mary, is of us. The Solemnity of Mary is a cataclysmic theology of both the compassion of God for human limitation and the potential of the human spirit to grow into the divine.

EPIPHANY

The second great feast of the Christmas season that amplifies our awareness of the person of Jesus is the Western church's separate celebration of the ancient Eastern feast of the Epiphany. While the Eastern church concentrates on the baptism of Jesus as the divine revelation of the holy Trinity, the Western church continues to maintain the story of the Magi. These foreign kings, themselves alerted by strange manifestations of the stars in the heavens, like the shepherds, find their way to the Child and, the Scriptures say, "to pay him homage" (Matt. 2:2). The world recognizes the heavenly in this tiny Child. And the Child recognizes the people of God in them. This is not a Christian child only; this Child belongs to the world.

THE BAPTISM OF JESUS

On the Sunday after Epiphany, the Christmas season ends in the West with its own celebration of the baptism of

Jesus by John at the Jordan. As the Eastern church points out, it is at this moment that we see for the first time the union of God the Creator, God the Son, and God the Holy Spirit. But we see something else as well. We see Jesus accepting baptism by John, a sign that Jesus accepts humanity, His own and ours, in all of its struggles, all of its limitations, all of its burdens, and all its focus on the ultimate, on the divine.

> *Christmas is larger than a baby in a manger.*
> *Christmas is the coming of a whole new world.*

The feast days of Christmastide make the full meaning of Christmas clear. There can be no doubt about it: this Child is human, yes, but He is of heavenly as well as earthly origin. In this Child's light we all walk safely through the unknown. We are all here with the Magi, full of gifts to give in his behalf. What's more, with the opening of the heavens on the bank of the Jordan, we all have our first vision of life beyond life.

Christmas is larger than a baby in a manger. Christmas is the coming of a whole new world. More than that, it is what makes that world possible.

15

ORDINARY TIME I:
THE WISDOM OF
ENOUGHNESS

ONE OF THE MOST INTERESTING, AND PERHAPS MOST
meaningful aspects of the liturgical year is its commitment to both concentration and contemplation. First, it
focuses us on only two major events in the life of Jesus—
His birth and His Resurrection. Second, it refuses to overload either of them into oblivion. The concentration on
both is laserlike, quick, clear, hot, intense, and revealing.
But however important the message and the meaning of
each feast, neither of them is allowed to be lost in a
swamp of important but unrelated theological interests.

The liturgical year is designed to take us into deep contemplation. It is about immersion in the great mysteries of
the faith. It is about the life of Jesus as it intersects with our
own. It is not an arbitrary collection of feast days, however

enlightening or formative they may be. In fact, the church has cleared its liturgical calendar at least three major times in history, each time purging them of various popular or cultural feast days that had managed across the ages to make their way to the calendar of the universal church. The most recent of these calendar reforms in our own time evacuated the liturgical calendar of insignificant feasts once again.

The liturgical year is designed to take us into deep contemplation.

After the Liturgical Renewal of the 1950s, with its concern for liturgical theology rather than popular piety, feast days that could not be historically verified or lacked universal value were omitted from the official calendar of the church.

But the purpose of these reforms was for more than historical accuracy, as significant a move as that was in a modern, scientific world. The purpose of the reforms was to shine the light of the universal church even more brightly on those poles of the life of Jesus upon which the faith stands—His Incarnation and His Resurrection.

The time between Christmas and Lent, therefore, and the time between Pentecost and Advent became known as "Ordinary Time," time outside the seasons of the two great feasts of the church. Time to rest in the contemplation of those centers of the faith that are the lodestones of our souls.

These two periods of time in the liturgical year, then, are contemplative times. They take us apart to think about what we have just seen of the faith: the birth of the Word that would reach across the centuries, the outreach of One who would transcend the nations, the choice of a woman as conduit of the will of God, the call and commitment of one who was both Son of Man and Son of God. It is an awesome context in which to begin the contemplation of the divine and the adventure of the spiritual development.

In this period that is between the two poles of the life of Jesus, we get to pause awhile. To take it all in. To make the connection between that life, that reality, and our own. They give us time to contemplate the intersection between the life of Jesus and our own.

Ordinary Time reminds us that contemplation is the center of the Christian life. It is the place where the mind of Christ and our own come to know one another, where we integrate our concerns in this world by attuning them to the next.

A bit at a time, we begin to feel the great magnet of the liturgical year draw us more and more into the one clear message: in the liturgical year we live the life of Jesus day after day until finally one day it becomes our own. We become the message of it. We grow into the life of it. We ourselves become players in the great drama of the bringing of the reign of God to the turmoil of the world. We begin, in the end, to see that the spirituality of the liturgical year is not an exercise of private devotion. It is the journey from Nazareth to Jerusalem that takes us, on the way, to Egypt, to Samaria, to Roman soldiers and Jewish high priests, to the poor and to the cross, to total commitment and everlasting resurrection, to the heart of the faith and so to the heart of the world.

> *In the liturgical year we live the life of Jesus*
> *day after day until finally one day it becomes our own.*

It is in the contemplation of the mysteries of the faith, the deep-down wrestling match of conflicting ideas, that resides the motivating power it takes to become what we see in Jesus. The world around us tells us that life is about money, security, power, and success. Yet the Gospels tell us that life is about something completely other. Real life, the Gospels tell us, is about doing the will of God, speaking for the poor, changing the lives of widows and orphans, exalting the status of women, refusing to make war, laying down our lives for the other, the invisible, and the enemy. It is about taking everyone in instead of leaving anyone out. When we learn that, after years of being steeped in the lessons of one liturgical year after another, then life changes for everyone. The fruit of contemplation is oneness with the world.

Ordinary Time refuses to overwhelm us with distractions, even religious and liturgical distractions, regardless how pious they may seem. Instead, it keeps us rooted in the great, driving truths of the faith: Jesus was, is, and will come again. In those three insights is all there is to know. In that conviction we have enough spirituality for a lifetime. Everything else is in apposition, is simply a modifier, an explanation, an example of the truth of it. But that takes a lifetime of contemplation, of pause, of reflection. That takes an understanding of the value and purpose of Ordinary Time.

Once we understand the impact of the birth of Jesus on our own lives, we come to realize the efforts demanded of us in our ordinary lives. Then we are ready to begin the spiritual disciplines designed to strengthen us for the passions, deaths, and resurrections of our own lives. Then we are ready to approach the second great pole of the liturgical year, Lent and Easter.

16

ASCETICISM

HOWEVER RESPLENDENT THE SANCTUARY OF THE church on Christmas Day, however piercing the sung Gloria at Midnight Mass, there is another side to being alive, another side to the liturgical year. Life, we come to understand, is not only about joy. It is about the power to endure what is not joyful as well. What's more, it doesn't take very long to learn this. However much Christmas revolves around gift giving and personal indulgence, this part of the year, Lent, revolves around sacrifice. This part of the year is clear in its underlying message: God is not a magic act, not a vending machine of Christmas cookies. God is life writ large. This means that we must be able to deal with all of its dimensions if we are going to live it well. We must be prepared to give up some things if we intend to get things that are even more important.

I remember quite clearly the day in grade school when my teacher put a large box on the corner of her desk and posters of starving children around the room. Lent was coming, she explained to us. We should give up candy and put the candy money we saved in the box for the missions. These were the poster children we should be sacrificing to save.

> *We must be prepared to give up some things if*
> *we intend to get things that are even more important.*

It was a child's catechetical exercise, yes, but it carried with it spiritual messages enough to last for a lifetime. Clearly, we were being put on notice. There were things in life, other people in life, for which each of us was responsible, however young we were and whether we had any association with them or not. There were things in life so important, it seemed, that we would need to give up some things for ourselves in order to take care of the needs of others. And it all had something to do with God.

At the same time, the purple vestments—solemn looking and dour—came out in church. Gone were the bright white ones and the glorious reds. In their place, the sanctuary went suddenly dark. The purple coverings and liturgical clothes looked nice enough but somber, nevertheless. And so were the hymns and the readings and the homilies.

It was all serious now. It was not about getting things; it was about giving things. It was about spirituality become adult.

Austerity had become the order of the day. We were to eat less food, to celebrate less, and to pray more. This was clearly tenebrous time. This was time for weighty reflection, they told us. This was time for strenuous living, we could see.

When you're young, the act of giving something up for Lent is an epochal moment. It involves a complete revaluation of what it means to be human. If life is not about permanent and continual self-satisfaction, what is it about? And why? How is it that the notion of bridling the self can be as important as satisfying the self?

What becomes even clearer as the years go by is that this understanding of penance and sacrifice as part of what it means to be a spiritual person is one of the most ancient traditions in religious history. It is common to all religions; it is thousands of years old. In Christianity, it can be traced as far back as the early second century. Ardent Christians, monastics, left the cities where narcissism held full sway to live as solitaries in the desert in order to do battle with the enemies of the soul. They practiced harsh penances and purged themselves completely of all worldly pleasures in order to witness to a life beyond this life, a life beyond the gratification of the body to the single-minded development of the soul.

Over the centuries, thanks to a better appreciation of both the body and the material world, religious figures have been careful to curb the excesses of asceticism. The starving, wild-eyed holy man is a figure of the past now. But the notion that self-control is an essential part of the spiritual life is a basic one. What's more, it is also a psychologically healthy one as well.

The ascetic is the person who sets out to subject the body to the spirit. Athletes do it to achieve physical development and somatic control. They give up food and time and physical comfort to conquer mountains and swim channels and win athletic competitions. Spiritual seekers do the same things, but they do them for a different reason. Their goal is to conquer themselves and develop their souls.

There is nothing passive about asceticism. It is the active giving of the self—physical and spiritual—in order to concentrate the soul, viselike, on the center of life rather than on its peripherals. The ascetic knows that to become what we can become spiritually, some things—even good things, perhaps—must be forgone. It is not that good things must be forsaken; it is that they must be indulged in with balance. The Talmud says that "If a person has the opportunity to taste a new fruit and refuses to do so, he will have to account for that in the next world." The ascetic lives with the spiritual awareness that choosing between the good and the better is the discipline that makes us the best of what we set out to be. Asceticism is not about giving things up for their own sake. It is as much about achieving more life—another kind of life—as it is about giving it up.

> *Asceticism is not merely about giving things up; it is as much about achieving more life—another kind of life.*

The ascetical life demands that we deny ourselves physical pleasures. It requires us to distinguish between the superfluous and the necessary. It assumes that bodily comfort must not be allowed to soften the search for spiritual fortitude. Every religious tradition, as a result, requires that the seeker give things up, yes, but it also promises gifts of the soul that can hardly be acquired any other way.

Self-indulgence, the preening of the self for the sake of the self, blocks out the cries of the rest of the world, makes us deaf to anything beyond ourselves. The starving continue to starve while the self-indulgent feast and, full of the good things they have wrested from life, think they have done a good thing. But the spiritual seek the good that "neither moth nor rust consumes" (Matt. 6:20). They are the spiritual athletes of life. Enter the challenge of the box on the desk—the mite box, they called it—begging us to give money for children we've never met.

To be able to control our bodies is to be able to control ourselves in even more challenging situations. Fasting enables us to say no to ourselves, no small feat in a world that stresses self-gratification to the ultimate. Never saying no to the self becomes the holy grail in a world more intent on the material than on the spiritual.

Self-authorization, the notion that all life, all knowledge, all moral wisdom begins and ends with the self, makes us our own god. And that is a small god indeed. As long as we are the only monitor of our own lives, as long as we never bow our heads to the perceptions and experience of the other, we never learn the wisdom of the world around us. We become the author of our own lives—with all the error, all the smallness that implies. It leaves us heirs only of our own limitations.

Self-centeredness makes us the center of the universe. The notion that all things were made for our comfort and our control robs those around us of their own gifts. It absorbs the gifts of others; it smothers them under our own; it blinds us to both their needs and their gifts.

Learning to forgo the lusting self, then, is one of the disciplines of the spiritual life. But giving things up does not imply loss. In fact, because of what we give up, we stand to gain a great deal.

Through acts of asceticism, we learn the most difficult thing in life: we master the gift of self-conquest. We are no longer prey to our own excesses. Now we are in control of the most difficult material we'll ever confront—ourselves. We learn what Jesus meant when he said, "Unless a grain of wheat falls into the earth and dies, it remains just a single grain" (John 12:24). To become all that we are meant to be, we must learn to become a little less than we demand to be.

But asceticism gives us even more than that. It gives us the gift of contemplation to which Ordinary Time itself leads us. We become aware of what is necessary in life, rather than wasting all life's energies on what is at most cosmetic. We gain the kind of consciousness that is lost in the fog of alcohol or gluttony, agitated by lust, consumed by greed. We learn the greatest gift of all—freedom from the demands of the self for the good of the flowering of the spirit.

It is these things that the great fast, Lent, comes to give us so that, rather than being persuaded and distracted by the things of the world around us, we can learn to keep our inner eye on the world to come. The asceticism of Lent comes to train us, like spiritual athletes, to keep our eyes, with Jesus, on the road to Jerusalem. Then, perhaps, we will come, like Jesus, to see the sick and the lame, the outcast and the foreigner in our own world and bend to heal them, stop to listen to them, reach out to raise them from the dead edges of society to new life.

The asceticism of Lent comes to train us, like spiritual athletes, to keep our eyes, with Jesus, on the road to Jerusalem.

Lent, you see, is not about pretending to be in first-century Jerusalem; it is not about playing the games of the spirit. It is about becoming a new kind of spirit ourselves.

17

LENT: A SYMPHONY IN THREE PARTS

To understand Lent and its characteristic forty-day fast in its fullness would require a process of wandering back and forth between its historical evolution in the church and its gradually developing sense of purpose, whatever the nature or place or pace of its evolution. In the final analysis, it is significant to realize that by the year 330, a Lenten season of forty days was common in the early church. That in itself, in a community that was only granted religious toleration in 313, is of no small significance. We know, for instance, that Christmas was not a universal feast, kept in churches everywhere, both East and West, until at least the sixth century.[1] Clearly, the Pasch was the earliest, the most central feast in the Christian calendar.

Every Sunday for centuries, in fact, the Paschal meal

brought the Christian community together to celebrate over and over again the awareness of the mandate, "Do this in remembrance of me" (Luke 22:19). No doubt about it: history is clear. The memory of the Pasch, unlike the history of Christmas, was a living, vibrant one.

No rules, for instance, were needed to keep this community together. No laws had to be passed to maintain it. In fact, no regulations requiring celebration of the Eucharistic meal were written for centuries, and then only as the hope of Jesus' imminent return had changed from the sense that it would happen "now" to the recognition that it was "already but not yet." Jesus, the early Christian knew, was alive in the community even though His risen return as they had envisioned it was less and less sure to come soon.

> *The memory of the Pasch, unlike the history*
> *of Christmas, was a living, vibrant one.*

The Resurrection, the triumph of Jesus over death, they knew, had already happened but was clearly not yet fully accomplished. Jesus was not again present in real time. Until that happens, they had come finally to understand, it is up to the community itself to be the presence of Christ on earth. Until then, it is here in the Paschal meal, in the memory of the cross and the empty tomb, the

Ascension and Pentecost, that the Christian community grows more and more deeply into Jesus. And just as significantly for the world around it, it is here that the Christian community renews its responsibility to go on together in Jesus' name (Matt. 18:20).

The question is, how? And why?

The practices that grew up around the commemoration of the death and Resurrection of Jesus evolved from place to place over time. One single thread of understanding, however, linked all of them: the common awareness that Easter was not the Christian Passover, any more than Sunday was the Christian Sabbath. No, Easter was different in meaning and in purpose from the Jewish Passover.

It is this difference between Easter and Passover, this crossover point between one spiritual worldview and another, for which Lent is designed to prepare us. For the Jew, Passover is a sign of salvation, of "God with us" at a particular historical moment in the past. For the Christian, Easter is a sign of "God with us" in the past, but with us now also and at a time to come, as well. This single conscious concept is the life-breath of the faith, of life in Christ, of the Christian witness now and forever. Each succeeding year, Lent calls each of us to renew our ongoing commitment to the implications of the Resurrection in our own lives, here and now. But that demands both the healing of the soul and the honing of the soul, both penance and faith, both a purging of what is superfluous in our lives and the heightening, the intensifying, of what is meaningful.

Lent is a call to renew a commitment grown dull, perhaps, by a life more marked by routine than by reflection. After a lifetime of mundane regularity or unconsidered adherence to the trappings of faith, Lent requires me, as a Christian, to stop for a while, to reflect again on what is going on in me. I am challenged again to decide whether I, myself, do truly believe that Jesus is the Christ—and if I believe, whether I will live accordingly when I can no longer hear the song of angels in my life and the star of Bethlehem has grown dim for me.

Lent is not a ritual. It is time given to think seriously about who Jesus is for us, to renew our faith from the inside out. It is the moment when, as the baptismal waters flow on every Easter Vigil altar, we return to the baptismal font of the heart to say yes once more to the call of Jesus to the disciples, "Come and see" (John 1:39). It is the act of beginning our spiritual life all over again refreshed and reoriented.

Lent is not a ritual. It is time given to think seriously about who Jesus is for us, to renew our faith from the inside out.

Steeped in the consciousness of the cross of Christ, the Christian goes again to the tomb of the heart, stripped of its distractions and lusts, to say, "I believe."

The question is, how should this be done?

Some say that the Eastern Christian practice of fasting emerged out of respect for the forty-day fast of Jesus Himself when, Scripture teaches, after His baptism in the Jordan, "the Spirit immediately drove him out into the wilderness. He was in the wilderness forty days" (Mark 1:12–13).[2] Others say the Lenten practice in the West developed in response to Jesus' own words, "Can the wedding guests fast while the bridegroom is with them? As long as they have the bridegroom with them, they cannot fast. The days will come when the bridegroom is taken away from them, and then they will fast in that day" (Mark 2:19–20 ESV).[3]

Whatever the theological impulse that drives the practice in Christian history, the truth is that the asceticism of fasting is common to every major religious tradition because it exposes to seekers the distance between self-control and the compulsion to self-satisfaction. There is nothing like a touch of voluntary hunger—the unsatisfied compulsion to seek comfort food, to bask in self-indulgence, to demand constant physical fulfillment—to give an edge to the capacity for spiritual concentration. Acuity of soul and consciousness of a life beyond the material come more easily when the material is not allowed to smother us. Lent enables us to face ourselves, to see the weak places, to touch the wounds in our own soul, and to determine to try once more to live beyond our lowest aspirations.

Acuity of soul and consciousness of a life beyond the material come more easily when the material is not allowed to smother us.

Having conquered our impulses for the immediate, having tamed our desires for the physical, perhaps we will be able to bring ourselves to rise above the greed that consumes us. Maybe we will be able to control the anger that is a veil between us and the face of God. Perhaps we will have reason now to forswear the pride that is a barrier to growth. Possibly we will learn to foreswear the lust that denies us the freeing grace of simplicity. Maybe we will even find the energy to fight the sloth that deters us from making spiritual progress, the gluttony that ties us to our bellies, and the envy that makes it impossible for us to be joyful givers of the gifts we have been given.

Lent is the period in which, learning to abstain from adoring at the shrine of the self, we come to see beyond the divinity we have made of ourselves to the divine will for all the world.

18

ASH WEDNESDAY AND
THE VOICES OF LENT

I GREW UP ATTACHED TO AN IRISH-AMERICAN FAMily with all the cultural elements that implied: most of the Irish men my grandfather's age, for instance, were railroaders and policemen. The women my grandmother's age were bearers of large numbers of children, many of them stillborn. Like the other immigrants around them, the Irish told stories of the discrimination and poverty that came with leaving one world and trying to fit into another.

One more thing they had in common: they all spoke about Ireland in the present tense. As if they were still there. Here was a necessary loss, you could hear in their voices, that would never be repaired. They could not go back, but at the same time they would never forget it. Most of all, they held doggedly to being Irish. They gradually became American, of course, but they went on eating cabbage, hanging pictures of the Cliffs of Mohr, and saying the prayers and teaching the dances and singing the songs that came over with them on the boats. My world, the American world, like the world of everyone else, was a mix of races and histories and religions that the melting pot had never really managed to melt at all.

It seemed that immigrants of all ilk wanted one same thing. All around me in the Catholic ghetto-world of mid-twentieth-century USA, second- and third-generation descendants of people from around the world wanted to go back to the "old country"—to Ireland and Poland, to Italy and Germany, to Greece and the Ukraine—"just to see," they said. Just to see what it meant to be from the worlds that were their beginnings.

So, years later in Ireland, as I sat having supper with the locals in the village pub, I remember the shock of realization. *Everyone in this place*, I thought as I looked around the crowded room, *is Catholic. Everyone.* To an American, it seemed impossible to be in a public place where everyone in the room shared one ancestry, one place, one common history. These were people with an identity that hung like glue around them. If they heard a name, they knew instantly where the family was from, what they did for a living, to whom they were related, and what parish they went to every Sunday. Their roots were living roots. They were not cut off from their ancestry; they drew from living water.

I realized as time went by that the spiritual life has something of the same quality to it. A good spiritual life connects us to where we come from, even in the midst of where we are now. It gives us roots. It carries a tradition on its back. It ties us to the past in a way that enables us to know who we are in the present. It is the place we never really leave because being there together is what makes us who we are today. That's what Lent does for us. It's about reaching back to remember who we are even while we keep on becoming more than we were.

> *A good spiritual life connects us to where we come from,*
> *even in the midst of where we are now. It gives us roots.*

The ancient is a compelling force in history, both public and personal. Where we came from, who we are, what our origins say about the kind of people we come from, what our history and monuments and holidays say about the kind of people we are meant to be—these have a hold on our souls like few other of the intangibles in life. All our lives we make great efforts to go back in time, to catch another glimpse of ourselves, to trace what it is that has formed us, to stay the same even while we change.

In a rootless society such as ours, a society formed by wave after wave of immigrants into a kind of hybrid nation, both ethnic and religious, genesis is an even more sacred part of the mental landscape we call the self. Mobility, in this new world, mixes us like isolated pebbles on a beach driven by winds and waves of long ago, unseen, unknown, unrecognized.

But not for Christians.

Christians have the kind of pith that grows fresh under their feet Sunday after Sunday, year after year, season after season, place after place. They have family far beyond the bloodlines of a place. They have ancient, basal roots to which to cling for sustenance, for nourishment, for depth, for growth, for insight.

Lent is one of those elements of Christian practice that binds the Christian community to one another and to its beginnings. It ties us to the core of us that is not transient, that is not changing, that does not fail us. Lent gives the lie to isolation. We are not alone. We walk with the church throughout the world on this journey to renewal. We walk, too, with the One who has gone before us to bring us home again.

Lent is one of those elements of Christian practice that binds the Christian community to one another and to its beginnings.

Every year, Ash Wednesday calls us back to the paths from which we have strayed, refocuses our attention on both the way and the goal of our journey through life. Every year the Sundays of Lent plunge us into the center of the faith, reminding us of who we are and who we must become.

Ash Wednesday, an echo of the Hebrew Testament's ancient call to sackcloth and ashes, is a continuing cry across the centuries that life is transient, that change is urgent. We don't have enough time to waste time on nothingness. We need to repent our dillydallying on the road to God. We need to regret the time we've spent playing with dangerous distractions and empty diversions along the way. We need to repent of our senseless excesses and our excursions into sin, our breaches of justice, our failures of honesty, our estrangement from God, our savorings of excess, our absorbing self-gratifications, one infantile addiction, one creature craving another. We need to get back in touch with our souls. "Remember man that you are dust and unto dust you shall return,"[1] the old Sacramentary formula warned us from God's words to Adam and Eve, as the ashes trickled down our foreheads. We hear now, as Jesus proclaimed in Galilee, "Turn away from sin and believe the good news" (Mark 1:15).

Ash Wednesday confronts us with what we have become and prods us to do better. Indeed, Lent, we learn on Ash Wednesday, is not about abnegation, about denying ourselves for the sake of denying ourselves. It is about much more than that. It is about opening our hearts one more time to the Word of God in the hope that, this time, hearing it anew, we might allow ourselves to become new as a result of it. It is the call to prayer, to liturgy, to the co-creation of the world. It is about our rising to the full stature of human reflection and, as a result, accepting the challenge to become fully alive, fully human rather than simply grossly, abysmally, self-centeredly human.

In the early church, Ash Wednesday became a time to wear penitential garments, to do public penance, to be banished from the church, to be sprinkled with the sign of human degradation. In a church more knowledgeable now about what it means to be "embodied"—to be gold dust in vessels made of clay—it is the moment of accepting what we have allowed ourselves to become and beginning to be all the rest of what we are meant to be.

Then, into the chasm of the Ash Wednesday heart, the voice of Lent every Sunday thereafter resounds down the ages to us, ancient, tried and true. "If you want to be my disciple, follow me," we hear the voice of Jesus say in the Scriptures of commitment (Matt. 16:24, paraphrase). And we find ourselves in that long, unending procession of those across time who have set out to walk to the Jerusalem of their own lives with the Jesus who shows us all how to go there.

Just as the three-year cycle of readings during Advent immerse us in the Christmas story, the Sundays of the Lenten cycle bring us face-to-face with the Gospel renderings of Jesus' journey to Jerusalem and the Pasch. They are, we discover as time goes by, the framework of our own wrestling match with the crosses of life. Each Sunday of Lent presents us with a special insight into the stages of the expedition that is the spiritual life.

> *Each Sunday of Lent presents us with a special insight into the stages of the expedition that is the spiritual life.*

The Scriptures of the first Sunday of Lent in all three years, the story of Jesus' temptation in the desert, remind us not to be surprised at our own struggle with the will to have power, the desire for things, the propensity for the morally malign—all of which threaten to deter our giving ourselves to the things that count in life. As Jesus triumphed over the seductions of the world and the limitations of being human, so must we.

The second Sunday of Lent, the story of the Transfiguration and Jesus' appearance with the prophets Elijah and Moses, assures us that this life is not the end, yes, but more than that—that this life requires of us the courage of the prophets for truth, for principle.

In the three-year cycle, on the third Sundays of Lent we see Jesus commission a Samaritan woman as evangelist, cleanse the temple of its secularism, and curse the fruitless fig tree. To be alive, and to allow what should not be to flourish in our presence, is to deny what it means to be a follower of the Jesus who came that the outcasts of this world may have life—and have it more abundantly (John 10:10). We have some witnessing, some cleansing, and some extra work to do of our own in this life if we are to fulfill the gospel ourselves.

On the fourth Sundays of Lent, Laetare Sunday, we remember to rejoice, first that Easter is near and second that we have seen His works in our own life. In these Gospels, for instance, Jesus heals a man born blind, talks to Nicodemus about being born again, and tells the parable of the prodigal son. He invites us to open our eyes, too, to be willing to begin again, to forget the past—however bad it has been for us—and come back to God knowing that mercy is already ours.

On the fifth Sundays of the Lenten cycle, Jesus raises Lazarus, says the grain of wheat must go into the ground and die, and forgives the woman taken in adultery and saves her from stoning. The Word is clear: to follow Jesus is to live, no matter how many deaths we face in life.

Clearly, the voice of Lent is not a dour one. It is a call to remember who we are and where we have come from and why. The voice of Lent is the cry to become new again, to live on newly no matter what our life has been like until now and to live fully. It is even more than that. It is the promise of mercy, the guarantee of new life. It is the resin that keeps our souls melded to the Spirit within us despite the pull of chaos and waste and superficialities on our spiritual moorings. Lent is our salvation from the depths of nothingness. It is our guide to the more of life.

19

SUFFERING

"SUFFERING IS NOT A PUNISHMENT," ROBERT Ingersoll wrote, "it is a result."[1] Suffering, we learn as we go, is the price we pay to bring life to fullness, both for others and for ourselves. It is not to be desired in a neurotic kind of way, but it is definitely not to be denied. For when we refuse to suffer, we refuse to grow. Suffering requires us to stretch our souls to the boundaries of personal growth. It brings to the surface in us both strengths and weaknesses we could never, in any other way, know we have. It is not about surrendering ourselves to pain left devoid of meaning. It is about finding meaning in the center of the self whatever the stresses around us.

Who does not know that growth is a painful thing? It overspreads and sucks out the heart of us. It twists us from one amorphous spiritual mass to another. It shapes and reshapes us until, at last, we come to full stature, to total development. It tugs us from small to larger, from broad to deep. Most of all, perhaps, growth wisens us. What we grow through, we come out of with a different, a better, a clearer perspective. We come to understand that every phase of life is to be won by dint of hard labor and great risk. Suffering is not nothing in the living of a life. It takes us to the brink of the self and makes us walk back, wiser and more certain of both our priorities and our principles.

The liturgical year sets out to do that for us spiritually. It takes us from one growth point of soul to the next until we come to understand the meaning of the moment, until we come to realize that the life of Jesus is the template of our own. If we are really meant to follow Jesus, then we must follow Jesus into every dimension of life, including into the suffering that is the price of it. We must look closely at how He handles each moment of life, what He expects in every situation, whom He helps, whom He chides, what He holds out as the ideal. Indeed, the life of Jesus is not a monument to the past; it is an invitation to the fullness of our own futures.

> *The life of Jesus is not a monument to the past;*
> *it is an invitation to the fullness of our own futures.*

The problem is that we resist suffering with might and main. There is a natural inertia built into the human condition that seeks the comfortable, the familiar, the secure. We want to shape life to our specifications and fix it there. We want stability. When life becomes difficult, the temptation is to want to reach the summits we can see, to settle down there, to turn our worlds into stone. We fossilize our hearts. We say this is enough. We limit our vision to what we can grasp without strain. We spend life trying to settle down, satisfied with where we've come, in control of where we are. Ironically, it is stability—homeostasis, the failure to adjust, to grow, to change—that threatens to destroy the very system it sets out to save.

Living life suspended over time simply does not work. The static kills. Only the capacity to go on living, to face all of life as it is, grows us. With or without our permission, with or without our understanding, eventually suffering comes. Then the question is only how to endure it, how to accept it, how to cope with it, how to turn it from dross to gleam.

Lent, the liturgical year shows us, is about the holiness that suffering can bring. It is about bringing good where evil has been, about bringing love where hate has been. It is about the transformation of the base to the beautiful.

But don't be fooled: Lent is not about masochism. It is about being willing to suffer for something worth suffering for, as Jesus did, without allowing ourselves to be destroyed by it.

Suffering is a stepping-stone to maturity. It moves us beyond fantasy to facts. We know now that everything in life will not go our way. We will not simply get what we want or avoid what we do not. And we will know when the price is worth paying or not.

The point is that no one escapes suffering. It is part of the rhythm of life, part of the process of living. The question, then, is, for what are we willing to suffer?

Because suffering is part of our mortality, it is important to spend it well. Jesus, contending with the leaders of the synagogue at the cost of His life, in order to bring the synagogue to the truth of its own tradition, we can see, is worth suffering for indeed. And many others, we know, have done the same for the sake of truth and justice. Martin Luther King Jr. did. So did Francis of Assisi. So did Catherine of Siena and Joan of Arc. There are simply some things worth dying for as well as worth living for.

To live for the lesser things of life is to risk not really living at all. Real life is pungent with risk, with the willingness to spend all the intensity we have for one great, lasting moment of creation—like childbearing, like human liberation, like being a living witness to justice and truth and love and faith, the greater things of life.

To live for the lesser things of life is to risk not really living at all.

It is not what we are willing to die for with which the Gospels of Lent confront us. It is not valor to throw our lives away on the cosmetics of life: the foolish drugs, the high living, fast cars, silly bravado, pub brawling. The glorification of that kind of suffering is not about holiness. The problem lies in being able to make a decision about what we will do that is worth suffering for. It is about living in such a way that where we have been is better because we have been there than it was before we came. It is living in the way that Jesus lived—for the sake of the sick in Galilee, for the women in Israel and Samaria and Canaan, for the poor in the temple, for those burdened by taxes in Palestine, for sinners everywhere who knew themselves to be weak and did not pretend to be strong—that determines the holiness of our suffering. That is the crossover point between sanctity and a sickness that seeks masochism.

Lent is the season that teaches us that darkness may overtake us but will not overcome good as long as we doggedly refuse to give in to our lesser selves, as long as we refuse to become the very things we say we hate.

Whatever the grief of Good Friday, however much evil plumes itself, in the end the apostles rally; the women witness at their peril, the unbelieving are converted; the living witnesses attest to the life of Jesus despite the danger to their own lives.

"The salvation of the world," William Faulkner wrote, "is in man's suffering."[2] And we have seen it with our own eyes. In the end, the suffering of Jesus is the salvation of the world. It is salvation of all those who see what is needed in the world and, like Jesus, do not shrink from pursuing it.

20

HOLY WEEK I:
HOPE TO MATCH
THE SUFFERING

HOLY WEEK, THE SEVEN DAYS BEFORE THE FEAST OF
Easter, from Palm Sunday morning to Holy Saturday
night, is charged with meaning. It is a microcosm of
Jesus' public life seen in bas-relief. All of its components
are there—the population at large, the temple priests and
their concern for orthodoxy, the prophetic words of Jesus
and the political concerns of Roman officials for the
social upheavals they feared could come from them, the
arrest and isolation of Jesus, and the fears and confusion
of His followers. Condensed into one week, all these elements in the life of Jesus are laid bare for all to see. It is
a dark week, a week heavy with the intensity of the drama
among them.

But it is also a week of two distinct parts. Palm Sunday—called also Passion Sunday, to signal the full reading of the Passion narratives in the Scriptures—provides the framework of the week. It reminds us that at the moment of what seems to be the height of Jesus' public acceptance also begins the process of His public betrayal, His public failure, His public abandonment. Only in the mind of God is Jesus any longer a success, it seems. It is the contrast between the laws of the world and the law of God that dooms Him. On Palm Sunday, we are forced to remember the distance between apparent public success and personal commitment. Jesus stays the course to the end, we see, and so must we, despite all other pressures, both internal and social, to the contrary. Here in the Passion narrative, we trace the struggle, one scene at a time, between the Word of God and the ways of the world.

We see all the forces of evil collude and collide. We watch as Jesus, caught in the grip of religious and political agendas, goes on speaking out, doing good, regardless. No political spin here. Then, in the first part of the week—Monday, Tuesday, and Wednesday—we get a glimpse into what will happen as a result. Jesus will die, yes, but not only. There is more than death to come.

All in all, it is a week that brings us face-to-face with the great question, why must this happen? What is all this suffering about? But deep down inside of us, we already know what the life of Jesus and these first days of Holy Week confirm: there are some things worth living for, even if we find ourselves having to die for them as well.

> *These first days of Holy Week confirm: there are some things worth living for, even if we find ourselves having to die for them as well.*

We suffer things we would rather not undergo because we realize that if we fail to endure them, we can never achieve what we want most in life. People struggle for days to stay afloat after shipwreck, for instance, because they have families at home who depend on them. Firefighters brave death to save their cities. For the sake of the new life to which they are giving birth, women endure long, hard labor pains rather than seek medications to allay their own suffering. To be able to see a worthy relationship between the sufferings we face and the fulfillment of the human vision is to be able to bear almost unimaginable amounts of suffering. Knowing why we choose to suffer is what makes suffering bearable.

The liturgies of Holy Monday, Holy Tuesday, and Holy Wednesday do not yet immerse us in the suffering of the week. Instead, they concentrate us on the future that impels it. Jesus is about to die, Monday's anointing story hints (John 12:1–8). But death is not the end, the Scriptures show us in John's rendering of the Last Supper on Tuesday, when Jesus promises, "I will go but you will come after me" (John 13:36, paraphrase). Clearly, death is not final for any of us. There is life to come after the Passion, despite the death of the body. There is nothing to despair, because this is not the destruction of the work. There is a time beyond time, the Scriptures imply, that makes all the struggles of time worth it. There is nothing to doubt, because the best is yet to come.

Most of all, the scriptures of the opening days of Holy Week prepare us in another way for the approaching end of Jesus' life—and our own. This way of life, with all its greed and enemy-making and multiple lusts, is soon to end. "Woe to that one by whom the Son of Man is betrayed," Jesus tells the disciples on Holy Wednesday (Matt. 26:24). Clearly, something new is about to begin for Jesus and the disciples. And for us too. Like the first Passover from Egypt to the promised land, we, too, are in the process of passing over, but from the end of one kind of life centered on the things of this world to the beginning of a new kind of life centered even here on the reign of God and, eventually, on the life of the world to come.

The scriptures of the opening days of Holy Week prepare us in another way for the approaching end of Jesus' life—and our own.

Life as we know it is not the reason for which we were born. It is not the purpose of our existence. This life, good as it may be, is at best the spiritual way station in which we ply our commitment to the Lord of the universe. The old days and old ways are ending; the new days, the new ways of thinking and living, are already here. This truth becomes clearer and clearer as we watch Jesus transcend the strictures of His time. We hear Him call us all to another kind of life, the fulfillment of which does not lie in this world. Not for Jesus. Not for us. Not for the church.

But the change from one way of living to another takes vision, takes commitment, takes the willingness to do what will be necessary to bring it. As Jesus did. It is this new vision, bought at the price of great sacrifice, to which Holy Week leads us. At the end of all the suffering we will see for ourselves with the women at the tomb, with the apostles in the Upper Room, with the disciples on the way to Emmaus, that there is life in death that is beyond all imagination.

The minor days of Holy Week—Holy Monday, Holy Tuesday, and Holy Wednesday—show us the end for which Jesus strives in Holy Week, the reason for which we ourselves live now: it is for the coming of the reign of God.

But it is in the second part of Holy Week where we see the price to be paid for the bringing of the reign of God to a world where the self is in contest for the position.

21

HOLY WEEK II: FAITH TESTED TO THE END

AT FIRST GLANCE, IT WOULD SEEM THAT THERE would be very little of a specific nature to consider about the three sacred days—Holy Thursday, Good Friday, and Holy Saturday—that make up the second part of Holy Week and immediately precede Easter. The historical dimensions surrounding them are few; they are treated under the single rubric of time as a "triduum," or "three days." They are called by the church fathers of the fourth and early fifth centuries "the Pasch, the passion of Christ and his passage from death to Resurrection."[1] They are, it seems, simply a narrative secondary to Easter itself. They precede Easter, we're inclined to think, in the same way some see the introduction to a book—necessary to set the context, perhaps, but not really all that important. The triduum itself, the grouping of the three days, is nothing more than a linguistic device meant to signify preparation for Easter, right? Well, yes and no.

The fact is that without the triduum, each of these days now seen as integral to the full celebration of Easter could be seen as separate, isolated elements in Passion Week or even still part of Lent. But they aren't. From the perspective of modern history, meaning anytime after the fourth century, they are part of the Pasch itself.[2] They are, in themselves, a piece of the mosaic that is the very bedrock of the feast.

At another level, too, nothing could be further from the truth than to think of the three days as separate. To do that is to risk missing most of the feast. In fact, very little is more important to the character of the celebration of Easter than the definition of the triduum. Pope Leo I, in the fifth century, makes it very clear that Lent ends on Holy Thursday. The triduum—Thursday, Friday, and Saturday—is a distinct moment, part of the Pasch itself, not part of Lent but the very time for which Lent is meant to prepare us.[3]

The significant question, however, is not what days are in the triduum. The question is, what dates were they *then*? When exactly did what we now call "the triduum" begin and end? And why is that important? And what happens to Christianity if the dates of the triduum, as they are now calculated, are computed the way they were in first-century Jerusalem?

To put it another way, if Jesus died on the day before Passover, why isn't Easter still attached to the Jewish feast of Passover? Why don't Christians celebrate Easter at the same time the Jewish community celebrates Passover every year? The answer to that question is no small item of faith. In fact, in the church of the first and second century, there were two quite different ways of answering the question of whether Easter should not be inextricably linked to the celebration of Passover. The issue is no small problem, because the answer we give will determine the very nature of Easter itself.

> *Why don't Christians celebrate Easter at the same time the Jewish community celebrates Passover every year?*

One way of celebrating Easter concentrated on the Crucifixion of Jesus; the other way centered on His Resurrection. The one that prevailed to this day has made all the difference.

For Jewish Christians in the early church through the greater part of the second century, Jesus died on the fourteenth day of the Jewish month of Nisan—on the day of the preparation for Passover.[4] At the very hour, in fact, when the lambs for the feast were being chosen for slaughter. From this perspective, then, Jesus becomes the new lamb, the Passover Lamb—the Lamb of God—sacrificed for us. For these Christians—called Quartodecimans from their celebration of the fourteenth day of Nisan, the preparation day, as Easter—it was the Crucifixion, the death of Jesus as Savior, as Paschal Lamb, that consumed their attention. The theology of suffering and salvation, then, becomes the center point of the Easter liturgy, the character of the Christian community. For Quartodecimans, even the name of the feast, *Pascha*—which scholars tell us is derived from the Aramaic form of the Hebrew word *pesach*—they insisted was from the Greek verb *paschein*, meaning "to suffer."[5] They didn't ignore the Resurrection, but they did not stress it.

On the other hand, early Christians who kept Easter on Sunday, rather than on the fourteenth of Nisan, were just as committed to the Cross as part of the redemptive act of Jesus, but they emphasized the Resurrection, the glory of the feast, Jesus' triumph over death. From this perspective, Easter is not so much about the Passion of Jesus, the date of Jesus' death, as it is about the passage from death to life.

Possibly the two modes of celebration might well have gone on existing side by side, but then the population of the early church, which had celebrated the Pasch on a single day, shifted from Jewish to Gentile—and then a decision had to be made. Who were we exactly? And how did we know? Was Christianity another kind of Judaism, or was it peculiarly itself?

With the church no longer centered in Israel, in a Jewish population, the question of the date of the Passover became unclear. The Jewish community functioned on a lunar calendar, not the solar calendar of the West. Time was calculated from the sighting of one full moon to another—all of them indeterminate, all of them defined by the rabbis. Even the average Jew did not know the actual date of Passover until the rabbis agreed on the time of the full moon. That meant, of course, that even Jewish communities outside of Palestine, let alone Christian ones, could not really be sure if their celebration of Passover was in accordance with the feast day in Palestine. In years when it was necessary to add an additional month to the lunar calendar in order to make up for the lost days needed to coincide with the twelve-month year, it was often impossible. The farther away the community from Jerusalem, the farther away it was from the rabbis' determination of lunar dates.

But if Jesus rose from the dead on a Sunday, if Sunday was the regular celebration of this Resurrection, then to attach the Paschal feast to the dates of the Jewish Passover—which could occur on any day of the week— was to obscure the very meaning of Sunday, the weekly celebration of Resurrection. It was to risk the central interpretation of the meaning of the feast. It was to minimize the distinction between Passover and Pasch. It could even obscure for Christians the theology of eternal life, new life, over the theology of death.

Meetings of local bishops from Caesarea, Jerusalem, Tyre, and Ptolemais, among others, were held on the subject, and the struggle to resolve the question of which mode of celebration was really most in accordance with the feast itself went on for years. Some argue that only with the appointment of Greco-Roman bishops in Jerusalem, the first uncircumcised bishops, did the tension over the issue gradually disappear. Then, as hierarchical commitment to keeping the Passover declined, the Lord's Day—Resurrection Sunday—emerged as the unequivocal core of the Christian celebration, whatever its historical or calendrical connection to Passover itself. In 325, astronomers calculated what became known as the ecclesiastical full moon, as opposed to an astronomical full moon. Since that time, the ecclesiastical date of Easter has always been the Sunday after the astronomical full moon that occurred at the time of the Resurrection in AD 30, at which time the equinox fell on or near March 20.

Whatever the exact date of the Resurrection, however, there are theological issues to consider that are even yet not totally resolved in the Christian mind. The real uncertainty involves a great deal more than the date of the feast. As a result, the church has vacillated from region to region, from era to era, over whether Crucifixion or Resurrection ought to most mark Christian thought, Christian devotion, Christian spirituality, the Christian worldview. In one sense, the date was changed to assure the relationships between the Resurrection and Sunday. In another sense, though the Resurrection was emphasized by the change of date, the theology of the Crucifixion and suffering rather than the theology of the Resurrection and liberation is what got transmitted. Excessive concentration on the Passion itself, even by Hollywood to this day, has often eclipsed the great feast of new life, the heart of the Christian dispensation.

> *The image of Christianity as bearer of hope has often*
> *disappeared under the emphasis on the cross rather*
> *than being heightened by the image of the empty tomb.*

The image of Christianity as bearer of hope has often disappeared under the emphasis on the cross rather than being heightened by the image of the empty tomb. What a pity, for all our sakes. For the Jewish community, it became the rationale for Christian persecution. For the Christian community, it became an obstruction to the development of a theology of hope and the rationale for excessive asceticism.

One thing is sure, however. The question of the triduum, its emphasis and origin, is anything but unimportant in Christian history and life.

22

HOLY THURSDAY

OF ALL THE DAYS IN THE LITURGICAL YEAR, HOLY Thursday may be the most impacting. Holy Thursday teeters on the precipice of life. It gives us a glimpse into both the best and the worst of what it is to be a feeling, living person. It sends us careening between great joy and great confusion.

I got my first glimpse into the spiritual disarray that comes with being hurled from an emotional high to a bottomless low when my uncle died in an accident the day before his son's wedding in the local cathedral. The wedding guests were already arriving; the band had been engaged for the reception; the body was being prepared for viewing; the grave was being dug. Joy was at the bursting point; sorrow was overflowing. What were people supposed to do? Which feelings would prevail? And even worse, what if neither one of them could be satisfied that week? How did we rejoice with the couple and mourn with the widow and family? How could we both dance at the reception and cry at the coffin?

I remember that weekend as a microcosm of life concentrated into a seventy-two-hour period. Holy Thursday is like that. Holy Thursday is the day of gifts given and gifts taken away. It is an exercise in short-lived triumph denied and stultifying loss.

Holy Thursday is the day of gifts given and gifts taken away.

In my monastery, for instance, at the beginning of the Holy Thursday liturgy, people crowd into the community dining room, wearing their best clothes and brightest smiles. The lights are high; the tables are set in white linen and candles, red silk streamers run down the center of the table; the wine carafes are full.

In the center of the room, on a raised dais, sits another table—chairless and empty. Then, without warning, the choir starts; the greeting is given; the presider mounts the dais to the empty table and begins the prayers of the liturgy. It is an exciting moment. The awareness of the Eucharistic community gathered together in one life, one action, our own Last Supper together, is overwhelming.

This night, when the Gospel reading proclaims the good news that from now on the world will be different, we see it with our own eyes. In the midst of the assembly, at each table, some wash the feet of the others, to demonstrate the difference between the world as it is and the world as it must be. Then the baskets of unleavened bread are passed, the wine is poured, and the community breaks into prayer and conversation. The Christian community rejoices, and the socializing begins while the remainder of the meal is served. Lentil soup, lemon meringue pie, chicken now where lamb would be, if not so expensive. It is all the touches of a Passover meal of herbs and lentils, sweet and sour, meat and unleavened bread meant to prod us to recall another Passover night, another people waiting to be saved, another people on a journey to new life. As we are now.

At the end of the Eucharistic meal, the lights go dim, the monastery quiets, and the bells go dumb for two more days. It is a solemnizing moment that echoes back through time to the Carolingian period more than one thousand years before us, when clappers, rather than bells, told of joy turned to sorrow by the end of the liturgy.[1] As the centuries went by, more and more signs of profound understanding of what is really happening here begin to accrue: A "fast of the ears" sets in, and organs are silenced. A "fast of the eyes" sets in, and statues are covered so that all concentration is focused on seeing only Jesus now. In 694, the Seventeenth Council of Toledo required that footwashing be practiced in all the churches of Spain and Gaul until, in

1955 it was finally ordered for all liturgical assemblies, not simply for cathedrals and abbey churches. No doubt about it: the impact of Holy Thursday resounds through the centuries. And why? Because conscious or not, the church knew that this day was the beginning of a new way of being in the world.

It is Holy Thursday, the first great day of the triduum, the crossover point between life and death for Jesus, between death and life for us all.

What is left behind in the residue of the feast is the very foundation of the Christian life. In this evening's Eucharistic meal we see the blend of life as it is and life as it is meant to be. Here is a snapshot of past, present, and future. We are reminded in it of life's present struggles and get a glimpse, as well, of God's eternal love. In the Holy Thursday liturgy, we sense the beginning of a Eucharistic world and hear the clank of soldiers' boots along a garden path at the same time. It is a private moment with the Jesus who has entered Jerusalem in triumph. But it is also a hint of trouble to come: "This night, before the rooster crows, you will deny Me three times" (Matt. 26:34 NKJV).

Holy Thursday is, indeed, a study in mixed emotions, like the accidental death of a father the day before the bridegroom's wedding. It is the sudden and intersecting experience of loss and gain, of joy and sorrow, of the tension between life and death—and all of them at the same time.

Holy Thursday is, indeed, a study in mixed emotions.

On Holy Thursday, the liturgy reminds us, four things happen that change our lives, that describe the arc of Jesus' life, that promise to change the world as we know it, that leave us all with decisions to make. If, of course, it can possibly penetrate our hearts enough to change us first.

In the liturgy of Holy Thursday, Jesus gives himself away for time to come. With the breaking of the bread and the raising of the cup, the signs of Passover blessing, and with the words "Do this in remembrance of me" (Luke 22:19), Jesus launches the passage that will take Him and us to new life. He launches the new community of which He is Way and Truth.

Jesus models a new kind of authority, a servant-leadership that ministers to the members rather than waits to be served by them. He does what, in that culture, slaves did: He, the Lord, washes the feet of the community. He does not use authority for His own gain. He gives Himself to save His community, to free it to function, not to dominate it.

Then He goes from that place to the Garden of Olives to await the fate that comes from doing the will of God in a society that claims to be religious but oppresses the poor, ignores the needy, and makes itself God. He goes, knowing that in giving himself away to them, He will lose his own life for their sake.

For those of us who sit and watch the triduum unfold year after year, as the spiral of insight and wisdom, experience and understanding grows in us, there is a decision to be made. Has there been a passage in us from old life to new? Will we accept what we have been given? Will we become what we are meant to be? Will we really follow Jesus or simply go on watching from afar?

The liturgical year, and the triduum in particular, brings us to the heart of these questions. Holy Thursday's mandate at the washing of the feet, "I have set you an example, that you also should do as I have done to you" (John 13:15), and Holy Thursday's mandate at the breaking of the bread, "Do this in remembrance of me," become the hallmark of our own conversion. No footwashing, no conversion. No Eucharistic celebration, no new life. It's that simple. Which is why we go away in silence to think about it.

23

GOOD FRIDAY

AFTER THE GLORY OF HOLY THURSDAY—THE institution of the Eucharist and the promise of a new way of being human together in the washing of the feet—the mood changes on Good Friday from triumph to horror, from security to fear. It is the fourteenth day of the Jewish month of Nisan, the preparation day of the Passover, the time of the choosing of the lambs for slaughter. Good Friday is the saddest day in the liturgical year.

Good Friday is the saddest day in the liturgical year.

Jesus, arrested and bound in the garden on Thursday night, is on His way through the legal system of Rome, we remember. He will be accused, jailed, judged, and executed. And it will be done—it must be done, the Scriptures tell us—before Passover. It is an efficient, even if unjust, system. It is, we know, the apogee of this final giving of the self.

But on this day, hope died. The One whom many had seen as the Messiah who would lift the yoke of Rome was gone. The One whom all had seen as some kind of wonder-worker had fallen from public grace. The One whom a few had known to be the Son of God had failed them all. The Bridegroom had indeed been taken away.

As early as second-century Israel, the pain of the loss was still fresh; the grief was still raw. After all, they were still waiting for His return, then and there. And in the midst of the wait, the desolation inspired a fast that tapped into the profound heartache of a people. For years, the Christian community fasted not only on Good Friday but on Holy Saturday as well. They fasted not simply symbolically or strictly but rigorously. For years, the fast was a complete one. Early Christians took no food or water at all. They fasted for forty straight hours without either eating or drinking.[1]

Pope Innocent I in the fifth century explained the fast as being in imitation "of the apostles."[2] However historically true that might have been, for a people who lived in the lingering shadow of the living Jesus—the First Coming—waiting for the Second Coming was a heart-rending task. They lived now only for the return, for the end of time, for the Parousia. Nothing was too much to do if doing it would shake heaven to its foundations, or at least bring the strength to wait even longer.

By the fourth century, non-Eucharistic liturgies, the veneration of relics of the cross, had developed. Christians gathered to read the Passion, to stand where Jesus stood in His agony, to be part of that agony with Him, to question their own willingness to carry the cross.

Every day the questions become more profound. Every day they cut closer to the bone. The question confronting Christians on Good Friday is not whether we are willing to have our feet washed. The question is whether we are willing to follow Jesus to the cross, to take up our own cross in systems that offer even greater rewards now for those who comply with the norms of the day than they did then.

> *The question confronting Christians on Good Friday is whether we are willing to follow Jesus to the cross.*

But now what is it about, this stopping of time on Good Friday? It is certainly not to wait for a Resurrection that has already happened. It is certainly not to grieve a loss we know will likely not be resolved within our lifetime, however much the Christian community of the early centuries assumed it would.

So why so much emotion now? What exactly is the

sorrow that blankets churches on Good Friday in our day that makes us all a part of the mourning crowd?

In many ways, the situation is much more serious for us now than it was for first- and second-century Christians. After all, then, in them, there was a living memory in the early Christian community of the system that had interrupted the triumph. These were the people who could remember the oppressors. There was no doubt in them about the extent of the suffering, the immensity of the inhumanity into which Jesus had come with healing hands and a kind heart, with hope for the masses and a dose of truth for the teachers of the Law, with a vision of God who wished them well and not woe, with another way—a Beatitudinal way—of being faithful. These people lived in the midst of the burning, real, present fire of memory.

In our own culture, on the other hand, there is the diminishment of commitment that comes so easily with distance from anything. We believe, yes, but often only remotely, only intellectually. We follow Jesus, of course, but, if truth were known, more likely at arm's length, at a nice, antiseptic distance. Imperturbably. Our commitment is not the kind of commitment that jeopardizes our jobs or our relationships or our social standings. No, instead, we are much more inclined to fall into the Passion-play notion of the Jesus of the Pasch. We go through Good Friday as if it were a modern version of a medieval morality play, something to watch, something to realize with a pang, something to admire. But nothing really serious. Which means, then, so much more important the fast.

The fast of Good Friday whets the need for the return of Jesus to our own lives. It means to concentrate us on the moment, to be there nagging at us in the midst of our distractions, to keep us keenly aware of what the spiritual life is meant to be about. It calls us back, gives a new edge to the life-changing dimension of these days. It reminds us that we, too, live in the loss of this Jesus who came and went and will come again, who was born and died and rose again and "who is to judge the living and the dead" (2 Tim. 4:1). Indeed, long live the fast.

> *The fast of Good Friday whets the need*
> *for the return of Jesus to our own lives.*

Good Friday afternoon ends with the veneration of the cross, one of the oldest devotions in the church. It culminates with the Communion service and removal of the Eucharist from the church. The songs of lamentation echo down the halls of the monastery for hours. "It is finished in beauty," the choir sings. Then, the darkness sets in; the quiet overwhelms us; the waiting—the interminable waiting—for the Second Coming descends into the middle of our souls too.

24

HOLY SATURDAY: THE LOSS THAT IS GAIN

Holy Saturday is a day nobody talks about much in the liturgical year. There is little liturgical data to consider—nothing really happens in most churches on Holy Saturday. In monasteries there is the morning chant of Tenebrae, a series of psalmic lamentations that punctuate the emptiness with grief and, by the ritual damping of the candles in the Tenebrae hearse, underscore the absence of Jesus, our Light. But there are no liturgical assemblies before nightfall. Nor is there even much history to pursue, with the exception of tracing the shifting of times and places and participants in the Vigil Mass. There are no public ceremonies, no particular liturgies to interrupt the sense of waiting and vacuity that mark the day. For the most part, we are simply left on our own on Holy Saturday. And yet every human being who has ever walked the earth has known what the emptiness of Holy Saturday is about.

Everyone who has ever lived, who will ever live, will someday undergo a Holy Saturday of our own. Someday we will all know the power of overwhelming loss when life as we know it changes, when all hope dies in midflight. Then, and only then, can we begin to understand the purpose of Holy Saturday.

Each of us will someday undergo a Holy Saturday of our own.

The importance of Holy Saturday lies in its power to bring us to the kind of faith the spiritual masters call "mature." Holy Saturday faith is not about counting our blessings; it is about dealing with darkness and growing in hope. Without the Holy Saturdays of life, none of us may ever really grow up spiritually.

Today, the church is empty. Today, the loss finally sets in. We sit in the empty pews, pass the empty churches, heavy-hearted from the reality of yesterday, of Good Friday and its dashing of our securities. Today, alone and bereft, we come face-to-face with the question we try so hard to avoid the rest of the year: how do we deal with the God of darkness as well as the Giver of light? Have we been abandoned? Are we left now on our own in this world? Is there nothing else? Was all the rest of it pure fairy tale?

*Holy Saturday faith is not about counting our blessings;
it is about dealing with darkness and growing in hope.*

The birth of Jesus, with its lights and organs and choirs, with its Glorias and its assurances of liberation to come, seems far away now. The Magi, with their cosmic promise, are long gone. The baptism in the Jordan and the voice it brought down from heaven have faded now, dimmed and muted by time. The healings of the wounded and the wonders done for women, the care for foreigners and the embrace of outcasts, have as much a taste of fancy to them now as they once did of truth. The triumphal entry into Jerusalem is, at best, a mocking memory. Before the new day had barely dawned, it had been swallowed up in darkness.

Where is this Jesus who walked the earth as we do still? The Jesus who understands us has disappeared from sight, humiliated, powerless, docile beyond understanding in the face of the oppressor. The Jesus for whom the stars shown in Bethlehem has been pressed facedown into the ground, all the Beatitudinal declarations, all the new vision of life for naught. It has ended in disgrace and degradation and destruction. The apostles are scattered. The community dispersed. There are no cheering crowds for us to follow here. Now we are on our own. We are left to ask ourselves what Jesus once asked of Peter himself: "But who do you say that I am?" (Mark 8:29).

The important thing about Easter Saturday is that it is precisely when its emptiness sets in that we begin to understand there is as much voice of God in emptiness as there is in anticipation. It is now, when we feel the absence of Jesus most keenly, that we can find ourselves listening to Him most intensely. All of a sudden we are totally immersed in what He has come to be to us. Now we see just exactly how much His life and words mean to us. We begin to realize that we have already been changed by it. What can we possibly do without it?

We know now that without Jesus, there is for us no bridge to God. Once we could hear in Him the very voice of what God must be. Once we knew, looking at Him, what we ourselves were meant to be, as well, if we were to be fully human at all.

Without Jesus, indeed, there is no way to take measure, even of the self. How do we know who we are without the model of Jesus by which to measure our own growth and goodness? What is hope when there is no one left now in whom hope can be guaranteed?

No doubt about it: this is the day of the going down into the tomb—our own as well as Jesus'. It is now the time for us to die to false hope. But it is also time for us to die to faithless despair.

Hope, you see, is a slippery thing, often confused with certainty, seldom understood as the spiritual discipline that makes us certain of only one thing: in the end, whatever happens will be resolved only by the doing of the will of God, however much we attempt to wrench it to our own ends. We have seen, for instance, how often what is dark leads nevertheless to the light. For some, there is no commitment to good until they have really experienced evil. For others, faith cannot flower until they realize that despair has not triumphed. So there is hope here, too, surely.

There is the hope that we will learn the meaning of hope, that we will give ourselves to the certainty that in the end God will work God's will, despite how much anyone tries to subvert it.

There is the hope that God is in the twilight parts of life as well as in its lucent ones, in the night of the soul as well as in the dawn of life, since both light and dark, night and dawn belong to God.

There is the hope that we will eventually cease calling only what we ourselves want as "good" and begin to recognize that good can come in strange guises, in shepherds and maidens, in fishermen and tax collectors, in presumptuous thieves and cowardly ones. We can hope to stop painting our world in our own colors alone.

There is the hope that we can finally find security in the fact of God's understanding of weakness: "Go and sin no more" (John 8:11 NKJV), we hear again. "Today you will be with me in Paradise" (Luke 23:43), we remember said to a thief on a cross. This is the hope that comes out of the icon of mercy as well as in what the world calls strength.

There is the hope that we can begin, finally, to see the world as God sees the world and so trust that God is indeed everywhere in everything at all times—in the abstruse as well as the luminous, whether we ourselves can see the hand of God in this moment or not.

To be able to come to that point before the beginning of the Easter Vigil, before the cantor sings the Exultet into the darkness, is what Holy Saturday is really all about. Then loss is gain, and silence is a very clear message from God.

25

EASTER VIGIL, EASTER SUNDAY

WHEN THE NEW FIRE BURSTS INTO FLAME IN THE darkness of our monastery chapel, it is difficult not to feel that this Christian community here and now has suddenly reached back across twenty centuries to that moment in time when the tomb burst open, the angels appeared, and life, for us as much as for those first visitors to the tomb, was forever and irrevocably changed. Only this time it is our life that is being saved from the inevitable decay of the world around us.

We are not, we know now with stunning awareness, made for this world alone. There is more to us than this. Life is about more than simply surviving. It is about reaching across the black void to the very reason for which we have come. We are here to grow to full spiritual stature, "a little less than the angels" the psalmist calls it (Ps. 8:6 DRB).

We are here to rip away the veil that separates the here and there, to glimpse the difference between what is and from whence it came, to be signs of the Light ourselves.

This is the feast of Resurrection, of the redemption of life from the abyss of nothingness to the pinnacle of creation. This is the feast that reminds us—invites us—to make the passage from one kind of human existence to another that returns us to the divine.

This is the very center of the church. This, not the birth of a baby, is the reason we celebrate Christmas. This is the reason for all the feasts of the church. This is the place from which we all draw our fire.

Easter, the scholars tell us, is the oldest feast in the history of Christianity, but it really only came into focus as a distinct celebration in the late second century.[1] Surely that's a strange turn of events for a feast we say is the center, the origin, the lifeblood of the church, isn't it? But not really.

The truth is that Easter, Resurrection, has been celebrated in the church every Sunday since the first week after the Resurrection itself. Even when the feast of Easter becomes a distinct celebration, it is only distinguished from the weekly Sunday celebration by the attachment of a one-day fast. Clearly, Easter was the lifeblood of this community, a weekly affair, not just one feast among many, however defining. Maybe that's why, in the course of time, little by little, it almost got lost.

Until the end of the fourth century, the Easter Vigil occupied the entire night. By the sixth century, the vigil ended before midnight and Easter Sunday now had its own Mass in the morning. By the end of the sixteenth century, the attrition was complete. Afternoon and evening Masses—the remnant of the early vigil tradition—were forbidden on Holy Saturday, and Easter began to be celebrated at dawn. With the loss of the vigil went the symbolism of dark and dawn, of grief and joy, of death and new life, of burial and Resurrection. The loss was a dispiriting one. Easter was turned into one more Sunday among many, and the church lost the experience of salvation, of commitment, of Resurrection, of communion with the One who has both left us and lives among us yet. Until our own time. Then, reinstated in 1956 and renewed again in 1970, the full meaning of the Easter Vigil and its centrality in the spiritual life of Christians began to emerge again.

Today, the Easter Vigil is actually four services. It brings us the service of light, the liturgy of the word, the celebration of our baptism, and then the Easter Vigil ends where the triduum began on Holy Thursday—at the table, feasting together, in communion with the One who has risen again, now, in us.

Here in this single service is the microcosm of the entire Christian life.

The striking of the new fire—the service of light—

comes to us from Frankish origin.[2] At first the Christian answer to the fires lit in spring by non-Christians in honor of pagan gods for the sake of new crops, it is still a witness to Christ, our Light. The candles of everyone in the assembly lit from the Paschal candle itself symbolize the risen Christ, whose light illumines our own lives yet.

> *The candles of everyone in the assembly lit from the Paschal candle itself symbolize the risen Christ, whose light illumines our own lives yet.*

We are reminded at the very beginning of the vigil of the One who has left us and is with us still—but differently. "I am the light of the world," we remember from John 8:12, as one by one the individual candles held by every member of the assembly are lit from the Paschal candle. "Whoever follows me will never walk in darkness but will have the light of life," we're promised in the same verse.

Then the cantor bursts into the oldest known hymn of praise to the night of Easter, the seventh-century Exultet. Slowly, surely, it becomes clear: we, too, must now become part of the Light ourselves.

The second segment of the service recalls the history of salvation by which we have each been saved from spiritual oblivion. It is the history of creation, of the liberation from slavery in Egypt. Then, lifted out of the dregs of life on the wings of the Alleluia again, one year older now, we know newly what it is to have been gratuitously saved from evil outside ourselves and liberated from the weakness within us, which, in hard times and on bad days, threatens to overwhelm us.

Then, in the third segment of the service, we are called to make our own personal response to the largesse of our God. Adults now, ripened by Scripture, tested by life, and redeemed from our addictions to the unrighteousness around us, we repeat our baptismal vows one more time. This time with the consciousness of experience and the wisdom that comes with maturity, we reorient ourselves to live the new life newly. Sprinkled by the blessed waters one more time in life, we find ourselves committed to try again to be what we are called to be. Most of all, we find ourselves in thrall to the One who has already forgiven us. "Today you will be with me in Paradise" (Luke 23:43) is a promise now made to us too.

Finally, the fourth and last segment of the Easter Vigil takes us to the meal of the Lamb who takes away the sins of the world.

Clearly, we have moved far beyond the night of the Passion that began the week to the passage from death to new life. We have moved beyond Passover to Resurrection. The fourteenth of Nisan, the day of the slaughter of Passover lambs that the early Jewish Christians emphasized as true to the Passover tradition, is simply not enough. We are the people of the Passion, yes, but that is neither all we are nor what we are principally. We are an Alleluia people. We are the people of the Lamb, indeed. We are also the followers of the Light that shines beyond the grave. We have come again to answer the question that comes out of Holy Saturday's emptiness: no, we are not alone.

The Easter Sunday morning liturgy completes the development of the Easter theology that distinguishes Easter from Passover. Just as the date for Easter since the Council of Nicaea in 325 has been based on the fourteenth of Nissan of the year Jesus was crucified but does not follow the Passover calendar, so does the meaning of Easter for Christians differ distinctly from the meaning of Passover for the Jewish community. The very nature of the dating of Easter stands as a mark of the divergence of the two traditions. Easter is always a Sunday, because Jesus rose from the tomb on Sunday. It is Sunday that is the Christian's Pasch, not Passover. Easter Sunday relates to the fourteenth of Nisan of the year Jesus died, yes, but it does not follow the annual designation of the fourteenth of Nissan that marks the preparation day for Passover from year to year even now.[3] Instead, Easter Sunday morning takes us back to the empty tomb.

There is a Passover here, too, of course. It is not the Passover of the "destroyer" that spared the Jews in Egypt and generated their Exodus to the promised land. This

Passover is the passage of Jesus from this life to the fullness of divine life. It is also, then, the passage of Christians from the life of this world to life lived in the light of the risen Jesus.

The focus of the day shifts away from the vigil's theology of creation and salvation history to unrestrained joy and wonder, astonishment and faith, mystery and trust. Easter Sunday is the moment Christmas points to, the moment the Passion obscures, the moment the tomb reveals.

> *Easter Sunday is the moment Christmas points to, the moment the Passion obscures, the moment the tomb reveals.*

On Christmas morning we find the manger full of life; on Easter morning we find the tomb empty of death. We know the whole truth now: death is not the end, and life as we know it is only the beginning of Life. There is no suffering from which we cannot rise if we live a life centered in Jesus. It is the empty tomb on Easter Sunday morning that says to us, "You go and tell the others. Now!" (Matt. 28:10, paraphrase).

26

CELEBRATION

ONE OF THE INTERESTING THINGS ABOUT RELIGION, about Christianity, is that in a society full to the brim with excess—a glorifier of excess, in fact—religion has come to be seen as one of life's great restrictive factors. Religion, this society assumes, exists to say no to the good things of life. It damps the human need for pleasure and destroys joy.

But nothing could be farther from the truth. Religion is life to excess.

Religion celebrates what the rest of the world forgets—the inherent goodness of life itself. Religion knows that life unadorned and raw is the ultimate high. Everything else is a pale shadow of the real thing. All the excesses in the world—sex, alcohol, drugs, gambling, greed—are simply substitutes for the real thing. They are made for people who have yet to discover the joy of being human, the glory of God among us.

It is religion, in fact, that built joy and excitement, happiness and satisfaction, abandon and trust, fun and holy leisure right into the midst of life in the first place.

When society rested on the fiat of kings and emperors, pharaohs and queens, tribal chiefs and keepers of the clan, it was religion that built freedom and feasting into the fabric of life. When peasants and serfs, slaves and captives, bondsmen and indentured servants all lived at the beck and call of the chief, it was religion that built freedom into the very calendars of life for them. Long before the five-day workweek and fair labor legislation, religion required rest and fun, fiestas and feasts, as well as fasting and prayer, discipline and self-control. The liturgical year, the church calendar, superseded the whims and fancies of either the obscenely rich or the murderously powerful.

It was the Jewish law of Sabbath, for instance, that built equality into the human race by requiring total rest for everyone in honor of the God who designed sacred rest into the very creation of the universe. On the Sabbath, no one could order another to work, neither citizen nor servant, neither human nor beast.

In the same way, it was the liturgical year that built both play and leisure into the Christian West. Sundays and feast days punctuated every week. All Sundays were festal, many of them solemn, all of them meant to honor the meaning of God's time rather than the burdens of our own. On these days, serfs and servants, as well as the lords and kings of the realm who could take luxury and leisure for granted, stopped to pray and play and renew their spirits and revive their souls. The liturgical year became the great humanizing dimension of life in periods when most of the world lived bowed down by the very pain of being alive, if not the inhumanity that goes with being burdened by the inhumane demands of others.

> *It was the liturgical year that built both*
> *play and leisure into the Christian West.*

Then the liturgical year served as much as a bearer of bounty and beauty to the world as it ever did of discipline and personal denial. Its feasts—first class, meaning obligatory; second class, meaning spiritually important; third class, meaning minor commemorations and memorials— all gave spice and purpose to life. They elevated time beyond the tedious and the stolid, the monotonous and the humdrum, to arenas of the meaningful. They made life with all its burdens the stuff of the ethereal and spiritual.

Celebration became the centerpiece of the church. In the monastery years ago, for instance, it meant the declaration of "recreation days" in another otherwise silent culture. It was the right to talk to the sisters you had lived with for years but never really got to know. It meant raisins in the oatmeal or dessert for supper or a tiny holy card on the desk. It meant that life was different today because days before us someone else had shown us how to live. It meant that joy, too, was both opportunity and obligation.

The church used the liturgical year to call our attention to the great teachings of the faith. It was a celebration of the ongoing presence of Jesus in our midst and the presence of God in the universe. It told us that life was more than life, more than the drudge of living it. In celebration we found a higher self, the whole person, the person who, as the psalmist says, knows that "the Lord is sweet" (Ps. 33:9 DRB).

The liturgical year sweetens life. It affirms human feelings, all of them, happy as well as sad, mournful as well as ecstatic. It makes room in life for feasting and for fasting. It tells us that life is a medley of sweet and sour, of the pungent and the soothing. It wakes us up to our own feelings and shines the light of faith on them. It tells us that being human is good, that we are next to God, full of the energy of the universe, fearless, full of faith and sure of more joy to come.

Unlike most other parsings of life, the liturgical year makes room for all of life. It is more than "fun" at any price. It plays, but in the service of joy rather than for the sake of purposeless idleness. It makes wide scope for human feelings: for fun, for play, for tears, for sorrow, and all of them under the auspices of holy leisure, of the contemplation of what it means to be alive, to be holy, to be God-centered.

To this day, thanks to the feasts of the church, the celebrations of the seasons, we are given the right to stop and take stock of the spirit within us in the light of the spirit of the day. We are enabled to put the work down and enter another phase and level of life. At least once every year, we are called to ask ourselves who we are in the Easter diorama—Nicodemus, the one who only comes to Jesus by night? Mary Magdalene and the women at the tomb, who follow Him all the way to the end? Pontius Pilate, who is so identified with the institution that he cannot begin to deal with the truth outside of it even when it stands in front of him?

Indeed, those who see the spiritual life as a life of restrictions and demands, of only yes or no, of life bounded by limits and denial, fail entirely to understand that the spirituality of the liturgical year is a spirituality made out of the shards and triumphs of life. It is a spirituality for the living and the joyful, the insightful and the wise, as well as for the suffering and the sinful. It makes of us the spiritual poets who see the beauty of life. In all its minuscule pieces magnified for us to see as we have never seen them before, perhaps—one rose, one windstorm, one baby, one tomb—life over time becomes, without doubt, one great, happy feast day.

27

PASCHALTIDE: THE DAYS OF PENTECOST

LIFE IS AN INTOXICANT NO AMOUNT OF MORE MUN-
dane inebriants—faster, deeper, more alluring, more cap-
tivating—can possibly equal. The problem is that for life
to become its own exhilarant, we must learn to live it consciously, to live it deeply, to live it to the brim, beyond the
visible to the meaningful. Somehow, in the midst of the
purely natural, we must become aware of what is more
than simply natural. We must cross the line between matter and spirit, between time and timelessness. We must
allow one to become the other so that the gifts of neither
may be lost, so that the electricity of each can be released
in us.

> *For life to become its own exhilarant, we must learn to*
> *live it consciously, beyond the visible to the meaningful.*

That kind of encompassing awareness is clear in the voices of poets whose souls find themselves routinely, eternally seized by a sunset, a single rose, the bleak sound of a nightingale caged and alone, the thundering crash of waves against cliffs too high, too dark to notice. It is obvious in the spirits of those who learn to see life more as a bridge to somewhere else than an excursion into deeper and deeper nothingness. It is, then, also clearly of the essence of those we call spiritual. These are the people who live on both levels of life at once, both the material and the spiritual, and find in them the unity that makes life worth living. These are all people who see more in the moment than the moment itself. These are the people who understand best the complex character of the liturgical year and its overlay of spiritual meaning on the materially mundane.

The impact of that kind of living is nowhere more apparent than in the liturgical year's treatment of that time we call Paschaltide, the days of Pentecost.

Here, under the rubric called celebration, is a treatment of time so strong, so clear, so encompassing, and in our time, so overlooked as to be one of the most impacting, most underemphasized periods of the church year. It is the season of Pentecost: the period of unmitigated joy, of total immersion in the implications of what it means to be a Christian, to live a Christian life. It is that point in the liturgical year when the curtain between here and there, time and eternity, for the most minute fraction of time splits open, and we begin to see not only what we are but what we can be. Better than that, we discover that they are one and the same.

We know Pentecost to be the day at the end of the Jewish Feast of Weeks—seven weeks after Passover—when the Holy Spirit poured into Mary and the apostles while they were in Jerusalem for the feast. But Pentecost has always been more than that, though often barely perceptible, as one or the other emphasis from time to time threatened to submerge it.

The Christian feast of Pentecost developed late in the fourth century, but it did not mean the feast day fifty days after Easter. It meant "the great fifty days," or "the fifty days of Easter." The phrase is an important one in a world that runs from one event to another, barely present at any of them. The word meant "the fifty days *of* Easter," not "the fifty days *after* Easter." This was an entire period of rejoicing. It was Paschaltide or Eastertide, not one day among many but many days of wonder and joy and new life all in a row. In this period of time, the Christian community has witnessed the Resurrection, the Ascension, and the outpouring of the Holy Spirit on Mary and the apostles. It was a time of great loss and great sorrow, of great demoralization and even greater confirmation and certainty, of Jesus with them still—but differently. It was a period that bridged time and timelessness, the natural life and the supernatural life, the material and the spiritual in one comprehensive and sweeping cycle of the Christian life.

Nothing else compares to Paschaltide for bringing the whole Christian calendar to one hot point of experience. Yes, the Advent waiting had been a glimpse of what it means to believe in the return. Yes, Christmas locked the human and the divine into the human psyche and soul as one. Yes, Lent brought us to our knees in the face of the awesome idea that the divine had reached down to us so that we might reach back. But only here in this time, between the bursting open of the tomb and, fifty days later, the overflowing of the Holy Spirit, does the full awareness of what it is to live in Christ, with Christ, and through Christ finally dawn. Indeed, these first Christians were the first citizens of the new creation. Now began the breaking open of the future. Now the human community sees life lived as it is meant to be. Now creation is re-created.

> *Nothing else compares to Paschaltide for bringing the whole Christian calendar to one hot point of experience.*

In this Creation, Jesus, risen, walks among the living to demonstrate the presence of the living God among us. In this period, we are all risen to new life. We all become a new people together.

Liturgically, it is a period of unmitigated celebration. There is a sense of holy abandonment to this space between the already-but-not-yet feel of life, a kind of reckless giddiness in the church year. For fifty great days, the heart of the Christian community has a sense of ultimate fulfillment. At the First Coming, at the Incarnation, we know possibility. After the Resurrection, till the Second Coming, we know the power of the presence of God in the midst of us. From now till then, the early church taught, the Spirit would companion us home.

> *For fifty great days, the heart of the Christian community has a sense of ultimate fulfillment.*

The consciousness of the ongoing presence of God overtakes us: we are not orphans. We are not wanderers anymore. We are not left to wonder now about what is really our fate. We already know it. We have already seen it among us. There is nothing to wait for now except for the waiting to be over.

It is a delicious time. A shaft of light has come to pierce the uncertainties of the seeking. We are living now with a torch in our hands, however dark the darkness.

For the early Christians—and for us now—it is a matter only of allowing the Spirit to transform us so that our life and the life of Christ do finally merge, do really melt into one another, do truly become one, are united both here and hereafter.

"Your sorrow will be turned into joy," Jesus promised (John 16:20 NKJV). And for fifty days we allow ourselves to be caught up in the consciousness of it as incomplete, of course, but coming, clearly coming. We are indeed now risen with Christ.

As centuries passed, the emphasis of Paschaltide shifted, unfortunately, from "the great fifty days" to "the fortieth *day*" and "the fiftieth *day*," the feasts of the Ascension and Pentecost. Ascension began to be seen as the proof of the divinity of Jesus, rather than as the movement from one phase of divine life among us to another. Pentecost itself, first meant to seal the meaning of the fifty days before it, began to be celebrated more as the singular feast of the outpouring of the Holy Spirit. But Pentecost, we are now discovering again, is much more than that. It is the period of Christian enlightenment. We come to know during these great fifty days not only who Jesus is but who we are meant to be, as a result. It is the coming home of the Christian to the spiritual self. It is, at long last, the comprehension of what it means to live the interior life in an exterior world, to grasp the real meaning of spiritual maturity.

Now the spiritual seeker understands the poet's single-minded search for the one thing that matters, the saint's understanding of the blur between the material and the spiritual.

The Paschal candle—Jesus with us—shines every day in the church.

The liturgical symbols of such liberation, of such fulfillment, are rich and riotous. For fifty days all fasts are forbidden. The Paschal candle—Jesus with us—shines every day in the church. We do not kneel at prayer, like fearful supplicants. We stand upright and confident, sure of the presence of God and already filled with everything we need to give this life meaning, to make it whole. We sing "Alleluia"— "Praise the Lord"—over and over and over again. It is a time of unbounded assurance and a sense of limitless liberation. It is hope and faith and trust all bound into one in us. It is the fifty great days of illumination meant to carry us across the darkness of life's divides.

28

FIDELITY

THE STORY CHARMS ME. THE PERSON WHO SENT IT
to me swears it's true, of course. But it really doesn't make
much difference to me if it actually happened or is
delightfully apocryphal. It's hard to forget, because its real
truth has something very important to say about the core,
the essence, of liturgical spirituality.

It could have happened to any of us at any time. In fact,
it does. The only question is whether we recognize ourselves in it. Or to put it another way, after being immersed
in liturgical spirituality all our lives, are we in the story or
not? The story goes like this.

It was a normal rush-hour day in a New York City airport. Commuters raced down concourses to make quick
connections between major incoming flights and local
helicopters or business jets that would take them from one
small airport to another in time for supper. Men in heavy

coats swinging heavy briefcases, and women in high heels loaded down with cumbersome shoulder bags skidded around vendors and carts, corners and counters in a mad rush to reach gates where the doors were already closing. There wouldn't be another flight for at least an hour. They pushed and jostled, bumped and pounded their way through a jumble of people dashing down the same corridor but in the opposite direction.

Suddenly, everyone heard the crash. The fruit stand teetered for a moment and then tilted the fruit baskets off the countertop to the floor. Apples and oranges rolled helter-skelter up and down the concourse. Then the girl behind the counter burst into tears, fell to her knees, and began to sweep her hands across the floor, searching for the fruit. "What am I going to do?" she cried. "It's all ruined. It's all bruised. I can't sell this!" One man, seeing her distress as he ran by, stopped and came back. "Go on," he called to the others still running ahead of him down the corridor. "I'll catch you later."

Seeing how frantic she was, he got down on the floor with the girl and began putting apples and oranges back into baskets. And it was then, as he watched her sweep the space with her hands, randomly, frantically, that he realized that she was blind. "They're all ruined," she kept saying.

The man took forty dollars out of his wallet, pressed it into her hand. "Here," he said as he prepared to go, "here is forty dollars to pay for the damage we've done." The girl straightened up. She began to grope the air, looking for him now. "Mister," the bewildered blind girl called out to him, "Mister, wait . . ." He paused and turned to look back into those blind eyes. "Mister," she said, "are you Jesus?"

For those of us who live in the rhythm of the liturgy week upon week all our lives, the question must be, so what? What has happened to us as a result? Who have we become? Who are we on all the rest of the weekdays of our lives?

We do not live a liturgical life to look good to other people. We do not develop a liturgical spirituality to affect a kind of spiritual dimension to our lives. And we certainly do not go to Mass regularly to avoid hell. We live a liturgical life in order to become like the One whom we follow from the manger to the Mount of Olives. We live a liturgical life to learn to think like He thinks. To do what He would do. To make Him the center of our lives—not our work or our money or our status. In the cycle of the liturgical year we learn about what it means to live a Christian life. We learn to distinguish the important from the superficial things of life. It's not a history book; it is the celebration of the spiritual development of the soul.

Liturgical spirituality is about learning to live an ordinary life extraordinarily well. Fidelity to the liturgical life is the cement that keeps us grounded in Jesus, no matter what other elements of life emerge to seduce us as the years go by. It gives us the sense of balance we need to choose between things spurious and things sacred. By its very unremitting regularity, it dins the Word of God into our very souls until we can finally hear it. Then, alive in that Word, we find ourselves becoming what we seek. It is fidelity that keeps us on the road when we would most like to simply sit down in the dust and let the world pass us by.

> *Fidelity to the liturgical life is the cement that keeps us grounded in Jesus.*

Steeped in the life of Jesus, we come to conform our own to it, as well as simply to mark the passing of another year. The liturgical year is not a history lesson—though it teaches us a great deal about the vagaries of history itself. It is a lesson about the ultimates of life, about the kind of faith that drives John the Baptist to the court of the king to announce the will of God and the women of Israel to a tomb in the midst of disaster. It's about the kind of love that takes in foreigners and gives away water in a desert. It's about the depth of mercy that cures outcasts and forgives thieves. It's about the kind of fidelity that keeps the disciples faithful to the commandment "Do this in remembrance of me" (Luke 22:19), long after that memory seems to have failed them.

Indeed, there is in this story of a blind fruit seller the echo of a Gospel story about a blind beggar. Those who have been immersed in the liturgical year all their lives would well be the kind of people who would stop to help pick up apples and oranges in the midst of an agenda that could seem so much bigger than those things at any given moment. "Jesus, Son of David," the blind Bartimaeus cried out as Jesus came down the dusty road, "have mercy on me!" (Mark 10:47).

The liturgical year sets out to form us in the spirit of the One who stopped and listened and gave new sight to the beggar's eyes just as the salesman in the story gave insight as well as money to the blind fruit seller. *Are you Jesus?* people ask us silently every day. And the answer liturgical spirituality forms in us if we live it with constancy, with regularity, with fidelity, is surely, yes.

The liturgical year is not simply about the facts of history. It is about spiritual reality in every age, for all time, and for us now. Then, redemption can go on and on and on—this time both in us and because of us.

29

ORDINARY TIME II: THE WISDOM OF ROUTINE

IT DOESN'T TAKE A LOT OF LIVING TO REALIZE THAT life is more than simply a series of highs and lows. By and large, existence as we know it is not a display of moments marked either by excitement or despair, by dazzling hope or formidable tragedy. It is, in fact, basically routine. Largely uneventful. Essentially predictable. Life is, by and large, more commonplace than exciting, more customary than electrifying, more usual than unusual. And so, not surprisingly, is the liturgical year.

Because the liturgical year is a catalog of the dimensions of the spiritual life, it is not unlike life itself. It, too, is made up of the habitual and the common coordinates of what it means to live a spiritual life. What's more, it is precisely this routine of holiness-as-usual that is the ultimate measure of the quality of a soul.

It is what we do routinely, not what we do rarely, that delineates the character of a person. It is what we believe in the heart of us that determines what we do daily. It is what we bring to the nourishment of the soul that predicts the kind of soul we nurture. It's what we do ordinarily, day by day, that gives an intimation of what we will do under stress. It is the daily—the way we act ordinarily, not rarely, that defines us as either kind, or angry, or faithful, or constant.

> *It is what we do routinely, not what we do*
> *rarely, that delineates our character.*

No doubt about it: the daily, the normal, the regular, the common is what gives clarity to the essence of the real self.

So important is this notion of shaping the interior life, of interiorizing what we commonly, even casually, declare publicly that we believe, that two periods of the liturgical year are made up of no great earthshaking mysteries of the faith at all. These periods call for no rigorous fasts. They develop around no overwhelmingly impressive feasts. It is simply the continuous, faithful, weekly attention to what it means to live out daily what we say we believe when we're at those mountaintop moments of the spiritual life.

Outside all the major feast days and fast days, outside the two great seasons and cycles of the faith—Advent and Christmas, Lent and Easter—thirty-three or thirty-four weeks, almost two-thirds of every year, is spent simply learning the fine art of living the Christian life. The liturgical year, we know, simply calls it "Ordinary Time."

But the truth is that there is nothing ordinary—if by *ordinary* we mean inferior or less important—about a period such as this at all. This, on the other hand, is the extraordinary period of coming to see the world through the eyes of Jesus. It is the period when we determine how we ourselves will act from now on. It is the period of catechesis in the faith, of immersion in the Scriptures. It is the time when the implications of Easter and Christmas become most clear to us all. It is decision time: will we take Easter and Christmas seriously or not?

> *It is decision time: will we take Easter and Christmas seriously or not?*

Ordinary Time, we know, is actually two periods. The first period of Ordinary Time begins the Sunday after Epiphany, the feast of the baptism of Jesus, and extends until Ash Wednesday in Lent. The second period of Ordinary Time begins after Pentecost Sunday and goes to the beginning of Advent. It is the time between times, yes, but it is much more than that. It is the period after each of the major seasons and cycles that immerses us in the implications of what it means to wait for the coming of the Christ into our own lives, to wait for the fullness of time in the next.

But Ordinary Time has an even more impacting effect than that. Like an echo off a mountain that ripples and repeats itself down the valleys of life, the Sundays of Ordinary Time stand as stark and repeating reminders of the center of the faith. Each Sunday, remember, is a feast, a little Easter, in its own right. Unencumbered by the overlay of any other feast, they carry within themselves, stark and unadorned, the essence of the Lord's Day. Each of them is Easter, a return to the core of the faith, the center of the church, the call of the Christian community that "Jesus is risen." Week after week we go back to the center of the system, not because there is some unusual kind of event going on but precisely because this is normal to the faith. It is Sunday, and we are doing this in remembrance of Him (Luke 22:19).

The Sundays of Ordinary Time are also an education in the faith. The readings of every liturgy for weeks take us piece by piece through the reading of Scripture. They root us in the lives of the chosen people in the Hebrew Testament and, at the same time, they steep us in the unfolding of the Christian Testament.

Scripture by scripture, they lead us along the path of salvation history and make us part of the crowds who follow Jesus from one situation to another. We go with Him from Bethlehem to Jerusalem, from the Galilee to Gethsemane. Now the One who was born in a manger begins to walk the byways of our hearts. Now the One who entered Jerusalem in triumph is mounted on a cross, is risen from a tomb, and sends the Spirit who is with us still. And we are catechized into the dailiness of the faith.

It is all designed, as the Vatican Council II directs, "to provide a richer fare."[1] Pope Paul VI writes in his Apostolic Constitution "Missale Romanun" of April 3, 1969, that the aim of the resulting new Lectionary is to make sacred Scripture "a perpetual source of spiritual life, the chief instrument for handing down Christian doctrine and the center of all theological study."[2]

Only four solemnities or major feasts are included in Ordinary Time. The importance of these is signified by the fact that they open with the saying of Vespers the evening before the feast day itself, unlike most feasts that are celebrated within the limits of a natural day. In each case they come out of a long tradition in the church or are an idea so central to the devotion of the church that they explain another facet of the mystery of the Christ.

Trinity Sunday comes out of the controversies over the nature of Jesus in the fourth and fifth centuries. The answer to Arians, who claimed that Jesus was perfect human but not God, is a clear one: there are three persons or manifestations in this One God, and the Trinity is the relationship between them. The Trinity embraces both the divine as well as the human nature of Jesus. The feast was finally extended to the universal church in 1334.

Corpus Christi, the feast in honor of the body of Christ, emerged amid the growing recognition of the real presence of Christ in the Eucharist. The elevation of the Host during the consecration and the cult of the blessed sacrament in the twelfth century were all by-products of the recognition of this feast that was finally accepted in the Roman calendar in the thirteenth century. It is the joyful celebration of the institution of the Eucharist on Holy Thursday, the importance of which is often muted by the tragedy of the Lenten triduum.

To this day, processions stressing the unity of the Eucharistic community are still very much alive.

The Feast of the Sacred Heart arose in the middle ages under the impetus of people like Bernard of Clairveax, the mystics Mechtild of Magdeburg and Gertrude of Helfta, Jesuits in the sixteenth century, and Margaret Mary Alacoque, whose visions raised the issue again in the seventeenth century. Finally, in 1856, Pope Pius IX made the feast obligatory for the universal church despite the reservations of theologians who argued against divinizing part of the body of Christ. Only the growing awareness that the "heart" of Jesus was simply the commonly used symbol of the affective body-soul relationship in the human being enabled the whole church to see this particular devotion as an idea of theological merit as well as an expression of very limited piety.

Christ the King, the newest of the solemnities, did not become part of the liturgical calendar until 1925. In an era of the downfall of monarchies and nations, of security and peace, Pius XI wrote that only the acknowledgment of the kingship of Christ—above and beyond any other earthly power—could really bring liberty, order, harmony and peace to the world.[3]

Clearly the human-divine relationship in the Trinity, the unifying force of the Eucharist, the mercy of God, and the lordship of Jesus bring all the scriptures of Ordinary Time to life. These feasts, born of popular devotion and theological thought, make Ordinary Time a time for making the faith the force of daily life.

> *These feasts, born of popular devotion and theological thought, make Ordinary Time a time for making the faith the force of daily life.*

There is nothing ordinary about Ordinary Time at all. It makes dailiness, stability, fidelity, and constancy the marks of what it takes for Christians to be "Christian" the rest of the year.

30

MODELS AND HEROES

"I WANT TO BE JUST LIKE YOU WHEN I GROW UP," I heard a young woman in her teens say to a speaker. "Tell me how to do that." She was eager, serious, sincere—and in search of a hero. The question is, how does anyone respond to something like that? How do we find heroes and discover how to become them? There are certainly many levels to the question. But one dimension of the answer is sure: hand them a calendar of the liturgical year.

We live in a generation unusual for its heroes, we say: Mahatma Gandhi's nonviolence drove the British out of India. Martin Luther King Jr., preacher of nonviolence and equality, brought integration to the United States. Thomas Merton, cloistered monk, led a peace movement from behind monastery walls and helped to bring the war machine in Vietnam to a halt. Eleanor Roosevelt, U.S. ambassador to the United Nations, made a role for women in international politics. Mother Teresa brought the plight of the poor to the sight of the world. Dorothy Day lived a life of protest for more than fifty years and gave the process of public protest both spiritual grounding and public intractability. She—and they—simply would not go away, would not quit, would not stop even in the face of apparent failure.

We live in a generation unusual for its heroes.

It was a time of daring and determined public witness. Hundreds of others like these around the world stirred the hearts of the globe. They changed things. They gave direction in times of despair. They gave light when institutions went dark with cowardice or corruption. They went down roads others had not dared to go before these women and men took the first step but where millions walk now because they did.

Witnesses to peace and justice, to truth and integrity sprang up everywhere. Nelson Mandela spent years in a South African jail but by his patient leadership brought a people out of apartheid. Four women church workers and six Jesuit priests, by their deaths, shone the light of the world into the swamp of evil inhabited by the paramilitary enforcers of Central American dictatorships and U.S. foreign policy programs. Women like Simone de Beauvoir and Virginia Woolf, Betty Friedan, and Bella

Abzug spoke out about the plight of women and led average women to the streets by the thousands to free their mothers and their daughters from sexism and abuse.

These people risked their reputations, their support, their friendships, their positions, their jobs—and their very lives—to give voice to the voiceless, to empower the people, to halt the machines of domination, even if it meant having to lay their own bodies down to do it.

The church calls them "witnesses." We call them unusual. But the fact is they aren't.

The liturgical year has always been a veritable roll call of people who gave their own lives to follow Jesus. The church called them saints. And that's unfortunate. The word has a foreign ring to it. As Dorothy Day once said, "Don't call me a saint. I don't want to be dismissed so easily!"[1] There is something about the word *saint*, obviously, that dampens the meaning of the mission. People like these were not marshmallow figures in stained-glass windows. They were the models, heroes, icons, stars of their times whose lives made real what Scripture could only talk about. They were the worthy and the brave, the simple and the centered ones, who saw the truth and lived it, whatever the cost.

The problem is that there are also those in every age whose leadership is bogus, whose life maps are warped, whose leadership leads to the grave of the soul, as well as of the body. It is in the face of these that the liturgical year mounts another kind of challenge. It is the Christian memory of the perduring power of the Christian message to rally people throughout time.

The liturgical year is about more than liturgical seasons, feast day cycles, theological solemnities, or a record of enduring devotions. It is also about the cloud of witnesses who have lived the life before us. By their very lives—in every era and every age—they prove to us that it is possible to be other than those around us who live to exploit life here rather than to grow in the light of the hereafter. They are about living wildly rather than living flamboyantly.

> *The liturgical year is also about the cloud of witnesses who have lived the life before us.*

Without role models, then, how shall any of us ever know that what we seek is possible, that what we want is doable, that what we are is enough?

The problem is that what society holds up as success, the Christian life often decries. When sexual excess is sold on every channel and mobile phone on the globe, what can possibly be used to dissuade the world from the notion that the violation of the other is normal? When greed is the basis of business, how can we ever teach the world another definition of *enough*? When society creates peer celebrities for teenagers out of addicts and criminals, thugs and dropouts, where will the young go to satisfy the high ideals of the soul? The answer is a simple one: they must be able to see something even better somewhere else. The question is, then, what does the Christian community have to put in their place?

Only those whose lives shine with the interior light that comes from refusing to waste themselves on nonessentials is any kind of adequate rebuttal to the prostitution of the human faculties for goodness. Then the Gandhis and the Kings, the Mertons and Mother Teresas and Dorothy Days, become the road signs of the age, living maps to another way of being alive. No institution can possibly succeed, however theologically or philosophically astute, without its models and heroes.

No theological treatise is any kind of substitute for the sight of a life well lived. No surfeit of incidental pleasure, debilitating and cloying, is, in the end, an acceptable alternative to basic goodness. Instead, persuasion rests, in the last analysis, on the presence of living witnesses to what it means to live well, to be productive, to make a difference, to grow to full stature as a human being.

> *No theological treatise is any kind of*
> *substitute for the sight of a life well lived.*

Clearly, the identification of role models is not an idle exercise. It is, rather, the key to the vitality of the living Word in the next generations. For more than two thousand years of Christian tradition, in fact, it has always been so. The question to us, then, must also be, what kind of witnesses are we ourselves being to those who come after us—searching for heroes, looking for models?

31

THE SANCTORAL
CYCLE

THE CITY IN WHICH I GREW UP, MY FATHER SAID, WAS
a microcosm of the League of Nations. When I look back
now, it's easy to see that the population was actually not
that global at all, but it was, at very least, a cross-section
of the greater part of the Catholic world. One part of the
city functioned on a civic calendar. In my part of town, we
existed on another one.

Our calendar was a collection of ethnic feast days that
flowed through the various sections of the city like a running stream from one end of the year to the next. The Irish
parish had a St. Patrick's Day festival. The Italians had a
street fair for St. Joseph's Day. The Polish celebrated the
feast of St. Stanislaus with a great parish dinner of potato
pancakes and pierogi. The Slovaks celebrated St. Francis
with a parish dance. The Germans had pretzel sandwiches

and beer in the church parking lot on St. Michael's Day. The Greeks celebrated St. John; the Russians, St. Vladimir; and years later, the Hispanics and Vietnamese and French I knew, all did the same, with some figure unknown to us, perhaps, but whose holy life shaped their aspirations and embodied their own spiritual ideals. Their parishes were smaller usually, more obscure, but there. Definitely there. And they all had novenas and processions and church banners to go with the feasts and fairs, the festivals and picnics that came round every year all my life.

These were the celebrations of the parish saints, the heroes and models who gave character to their communities. They were the figures from a holy past who had formed them and shaped them in the faith. They were the patrons of the parishes and the namesakes of their children. They were the honored parts of what Catholics called "the communion of saints," hallowed people now departed but very, very alive in the life of the churches whose patrons they were.

Saints abounded in our world. They were our friends. They were our heroes. They were our models.

I remember them all very well. To this day many of the saints still inspire me; some of them are yet to be understood, still to be studied for the wisdom they have to offer. St. Therese of Lisieux never attracted me much, but Teresa of Avila and her church-building visions captured my heart. St. George and his dragon did not appeal much either, but St. Joan of Arc, with her cross and army, fired my imagination. Peter, with his bumbling ways, gave me hope. John the Baptist and the fire in his voice rocked me out of my complacency.

All of them brought with them a heritage of struggle, a promise of triumph for the weakest of us. What they could do, mere mortals, so surely could we. While the rest of the children of the world found their heroes on magazine covers and posters, in films and sports arenas, Catholics added to them the statues and pictures of the saints. Every generation grew up reared on figures that stretched back in the time to the very beginning.

The canon of saints is as old as the church. At first it was only martyrs who were honored—Peter and Paul and those who had been persecuted and killed for refusing to pay homage to the gods of the empire in the periods of persecution. But then, as the centuries went by, it began to be noted that living for the faith could be just as holy as dying for it. Categories—characteristics—of sanctity developed. Some saints, the church began to realize, were virgins—male and female—who gave up the right to give themselves to this life in full for the sake of attesting to the fullness of the next. Others were confessors—those who witnessed to the principles of Jesus despite public pressure to do otherwise, like St. Martin of Tours, patron saint of pacifists, who died in 397, or Bartolomeo de las Casas, who argued for the full humanity of Indians in the face of a fifteenth-century theology that declared them only half-human.

> *The canon of saints is as old as the church.*

Eventually, the practice of having memorial celebrations at the tomb of the saints was, with the movement of the bodies to local churches, transformed into the celebration of yearly Eucharistic liturgies in the churches. The notion of "sainthood" evolved from being a matter of private honor into the status of public devotion. But other things changed as well as the church calendar with the cult of the saints.

Without common criteria for the naming of saints, local areas hastened to name their own, often out of local pride but just as often out of concern for the economic impact to the region due to the pilgrimages sainthood inspired. Over time such multiplication of saints' days threatened to smother the Christmas-Easter cycles themselves. At least as serious as the overload of the liturgical calendar was the fact that with the saints came shrines and celebrations, miracles and masses, hagiography rather than history in many cases, pilgrimages and relics for sale. By the thirteenth century, the church centralized the canonization process and took on the function of purging the universal calendar of local feasts and spurious entries.

In the sixteenth century, the Council of Trent required that abuses be corrected: "In the invocation of the saints, the veneration of relics and the sacred use of images, all superstition shall be removed, all filthy quest for gain eliminated and all lasciviousness avoided," the document demands.[1] As recently as 1969, the church dropped from the calendar of the saints those figures whose authenticity was doubtful, who were more legend—however laudable—than fact. The beloved saints Christopher and Valentine, among many, were eliminated from the calendar for the sake of historical credibility and biographical accuracy.

But the reverence for those holy ones among us who carry our aspirations for goodness from one generation to another—St. Benedict, St. Francis, St. Dominic, St. Maximilian Kolbe, St. Catherine Siena, St. Theresa of Avila, St. Mother Seton, St. Ignatius Loyola, St. Mary McKillup, and hundreds of others—remains, thinned down, yes, but cleared up. They shine like stars for all to see in the deep night of every century so that we, like they, can find our way home.

Is it an idle practice, this reverence for people of the past who took the liturgical year with its presentation of the mysteries of Jesus seriously? Hardly. Like the attempt of the young woman at the public lecture to determine how to model herself on a living figure, we all make our own heroes. If they are not passed down to us from the wisdom of the past, we will surely shape icons and guides out of the dust of the day that are far less lasting, far less inspiring perhaps.

In the lives of the saints, we see in our own time the qualities that make life possible. They give us the courage to go on when noise drowns out prayer and excess smothers self-control and conformity trumps Christian courage. They show us what character under pressure really looks like. They encourage us to stand against the power-crazed crowds. And if we hear their stories often enough, every year of our lives, perhaps, we may discover that thanks to them, our own internal core has turned to flint.

> *In the lives of the saints, we see in our own time the qualities that make life possible.*

The sanctoral cycle is what says to us that the call to Christianity we hear from a manger, a cross, and an empty tomb is as possible to us now as it has been to many who have walked that way before us.

32

MARIAN FEASTS

HE WAS SIX YEARS OLD AND NOT GIVEN TO CHURCH-going. When I saw the family at the monastery Easter Vigil, I groaned. *It's a long service full of dancing and singing, flowers and incense, bells and organ. Why would anyone ever bring a child to it?* I thought. But afterwards, at the agape, the boy was still clearly animated and the family was aglow. "Jake insisted that we bring him back here to the Mount for the Vigil again this year," his mother explained to me, tousling his hair proudly. "Really? Whatever for?" I said in obvious disbelief. Then the little boy looked up at me with a kind of mild amazement. "Because I like this church," he said. "In this church, Jesus really rises!"

Some memories never fade. The memory of one small kindness in a time of crisis can stay with us forever, can seal our bonds beyond all reason. There are memories that shape our very sense of self. We know ourselves to be "bright" or "fast" or "irresponsible" because important people told us so when we were too young to really understand what they were saying. There are also memories that mark a person for life spiritually as well: a special Christmas crib, perhaps; a particularly long and colorful procession, maybe; the smell of incense and the profusion of flowers, possibly. Whatever the source of the sentiment, it clings to the soul like dew before dawn, soft and quiet and amorphous. It is the mucilage that fuses mind and matter into one.

No one, for instance, ever taught us Marian theology in any organized, academic way. They didn't need to even try. It came with the May altars we built in grade school. It came with the crowning of May queens in high school. It came with the rosaries we said in October and carried in our purses and fingered in the dark before sleep at night. It was the DNA of religion in our bones. And it was all about Mary, the *Theotokos*, the Eastern church called her: the Mother of God.

Clearly, liturgy is not something created out of academic cloth. It arises out of the consciousness of a people, the needs of a culture. It speaks to the questions and concerns of every age and manifests to them in a common tongue the essential meanings of the faith. Perhaps that is nowhere more obvious than in the history of the Marian feasts of the liturgical year.

> *Liturgy is not something created out of academic cloth. It arises out of the consciousness of a people, the needs of a culture.*

One look at the changing calendars of the liturgical year across the generations makes it clear: Marian piety is part of the roots of the church. It is not only part of the most ancient devotions in the church; it has a continuing and present power. No amount of pseudosophistication or the best of liturgical theology ever manages to dislodge it. Holweck's late nineteenth-century record of 940 universal or local feasts of Mary leaves no doubt: the Marian liturgical tradition is one of the pillars of the church.[1] But why? Is it mythology? No, the major Marian feasts are idea feasts: they are grounded in a theology that is as much about Christ as it is about Mary. Is it superstition? No. Marian feasts that have emerged out of local churches or in response to particular events—as, for instance, the modern devotion to the Rosary that grew out of the apparitions at Fatima in Portugal—are just that: popular devotions. They are never defined as articles of faith. Is it bad theology? No. The object of Marian liturgy is not Marian at all. It is the manifestation of another facet of the saving mission of Jesus. The liturgy in honor of the angel Gabriel's appearance to Mary is, for instance, the feast of "the Annunciation of the Lord," not the annunciation of Mary.

The feast of the motherhood of Mary has nothing to do with the glorification of Mary. It is the church's answer to those who refute the humanity of Jesus.

The feasts of Mary in the liturgical year are a virtual catalog of the works of God in humanity and the collaboration of humanity in the Incarnation of the divine in our midst. She is, the ancient prayer reminds us all, "blessed among women." She is simply a woman like ourselves whose acceptance of the will of God changed the trajectory of humanity. The implications for the rest of us are awesome. The implications for women as women are particularly impacting. If God worked through one woman to bring redemption, how is it that anyone can argue that God does not go on working through other women as well?

Recognition of this relationship between God and humankind in the ongoing creation of the world is one of the most ancient teachings of liturgical theology. If it applies to Mary, it also applies to us.

The theological foundation for the revered place of Mary in the church began to emerge as early as the second century. Just as Jesus was the new Adam, the fathers of the church began to teach, Mary was the new Eve. Those ideas took deep and early root. But with the proclamation of the Council of Ephesus in the fifth century that Mary was indeed *Theotokos*, "the Mother of God," devotion to Mary as a teaching of the church spread rapidly. Local churches, both great and small, were dedicated to her; feast days in her honor were celebrated everywhere. She was mother, she was the Mother of God, she was one of us. Popular piety often outran the ability of the church to cull the ideas and define the concepts behind every new feast before they stretched the theological distinction between Jesus and Mary to the breaking point. The struggle to balance the tension between theology and personal piety was a constant but a dynamic one.

The present calendar of the liturgical year is the fruit of centuries of definition and redefinition that did not come easily. So powerful was the groundswell of devotion that the multiplication of Marian feasts threatened to obscure the real object of them. The church moved time after time to prune and limit the kind of multiplicity that could only dull the very dynamism of the devotion.

Most great feasts—like most great ideas—grow slowly, and from the bottom up. They spring up locally first. The feast of Mary under the title of "the Immaculate Heart of Mary," for instance, was promoted by John Eudes, founder of a religious order, in 1646. Not until 1944, however, did Pope Pius XII, in an era of World Wars and under the influence of the apparitions at Fatima, Portugal, extend it to the calendar of the universal church. And even now, after the Liturgical Renewal of 1969, it is at best an optional memorial. If groups want to use this title, they may—but, most important of all, they are not obliged to do so.

At the beginning of the twenty-first century, personal devotion to Mary is keen.

The point is that at the beginning of the twenty-first century, personal devotion to Mary is keen. But more than that, the liturgical spirituality that embeds us in the life of Jesus and the teachings of Scripture has been pared again to focus us on the role of Mary, of this woman "blessed among women," in the mysteries of Jesus. There are now, in the calendar of the universal liturgical year, four solemnities, three feasts, four memorials, and five optional memorials devoted to Mary, the mother of Jesus. They are:

January 1—Mary, Mother of God (Solemnity)
February 11—Our Lady of Lourdes (Optional Memorial)
March 25—Annunciation to Mary (Solemnity)
May 13—Our Lady of Fatima (Optional Memorial)
May 31—Visitation (Feast)
Saturday after Sacred Heart of Jesus—Immaculate Heart of Mary (Optional Memorial)
July 16—Our Lady of Mount Carmel (Optional Memorial)

August 5—Dedication of St. Mary Major (Optional Memorial)

August 15—Assumption (Solemnity)

August 22—Queenship of Mary (Memorial)

September 8—Birth of Mary (Feast)

September 15—Our Lady of Sorrows (Memorial)

October 7—Our Lady of the Rosary (Memorial)

November 21—Presentation of Mary (Memorial)

December 8—Immaculate Conception (Solemnity)

December 12—Our Lady of Guadalupe (Feast)

As Pope Paul VI wrote, "With the passage of centuries, the faithful have become accustomed to so many special religious devotions that the principal mysteries of redemption have lost their proper place."[2]

The proper place for devotion to Mary is a clear one: she is the mother, the woman, the human participant in the work of redemption by her Son. She is the one who heard the Word of God in her heart and followed it to the end, whatever the cost to herself. By her unconditional fiat, she became the perfect recipient of God's will that each of us would like to be. Her life belongs not simply to her own life but to the life of the world as well.

It is in Mary that we see God's creative will being done.

It is in Mary that we see God's creative will being done. In her, God not only prevails over the inherent weakness of mortality but brings it to the fullness of life for all our sakes. In the memories of the May altars, the crowning of May queens, and the droning of a thousand decades of the Rosary, all those ideas came to life in me and generations of others, came to heart in us, came to stay forever— whatever the titles given to those feasts as time goes by.

33

EPILOGUE

LIKE A GREAT WATERWHEEL, THE LITURGICAL YEAR goes on relentlessly irrigating our souls, softening the ground of our hearts, nourishing the soil of our lives until the seed of the Word of God itself begins to grow in us, comes to fruit in us, ripens in us the spiritual journey of a lifetime. So goes the liturgical year through all the days of our lives. It concentrates us on the two great poles of the faith—the birth and death of Jesus of Nazareth. But as Christmas and Easter trace the life of Jesus for us from beginning to end, the liturgical year does even more: it also challenges our own life and vision and sense of meaning.

Both a guide to greater spiritual maturity and a path to a deepened spiritual life, the liturgical year leads us through all the great questions of faith as it goes. It rehearses the dimensions of life over and over for us all the years of our days. It leads us back again and again to reflect on the great moments of the life of Jesus and so to apply them to our own.

Each church year moves with measured rhythm in order to knit Jesus' life and vision into our own personal journeys through time. As Jesus goes from glory to Golgotha, so do we all. The only question is, what shall we become because of it, as a result of it, in the process of it?

As the liturgical year goes on every day of our lives, every season of every year, tracing the steps of Jesus from Bethlehem to Jerusalem, so does our own life move back and forth between our own beginnings and endings, between our own struggles and triumphs, between the rush of acclamation and the crush of abandonment. It is the link between these two, the nexus of this companion-ship between Jesus and me, between this life and the next, between me and the world around me, that is the gift of the liturgical year.

The meaning and message of the liturgical year is the bedrock on which we strike our own life direction. Rooted in the Resurrection promise of the liturgical year, whatever the weight of our own pressures, we maintain the course. We trust in the future we cannot see and do only know because we have celebrated the death and Resurrection of Jesus year after year after year. In His new life we rest our own.

Every season of the liturgical year, every element of its

movement through time probes and prods us to embrace its ideals and purpose, its questions and answers, its reflections and its model of life. The liturgical year is not a matter of recollection and ritual. It is the eternally spiritual dynamic. It is the movement through calendar time of Jesus and the development of Christian community. It is also, then, the passage that maps the relationship of Jesus with me, the growing bond between master and disciple, the gradual adherence of the neophyte soul with the Spirit that drives it.

The tides of the liturgical year wash us back and forth between its eddies—one season flowing with joy, the next with sorrow, the third with triumph, all of which call us to our own new beginnings. In Ordinary Time we reflect on the meaning and messages of these liturgical seasons. Like Mary, we go through Ordinary Time "pondering these things in our heart." We grow into them. We grow through them. And in the course of it, we are given to see the footprints of those who have lived into it before us.

The saints of the tradition have made it real for the world age after age. They are the concrete examples given us to understand what it really means to live out the Christian vision. They are the prophetic manifestation in time of the eternal will of God. We remember in them, too, the history of the faith as it is forever reflected through the lives of those in the sanctoral cycle. They are those who lead us all the way back to the life of the One who was like us in all things except sin (Heb. 4:15).

In the idea feasts and solemnities, we revisit the great mysteries of the faith, such as the Trinity and Corpus Christi, Christ the King and the Sacred Heart. These feasts, like the stained-glass windows of the church, focus us on the spiritual implications the historical life of Jesus leaves behind for us to absorb.

Finally, in the Marian feasts of every year, we refuse to forget the humanity of Jesus and the role of womanhood in the economy of salvation, however yet unfinished.

Celebrating the liturgical year immerses us constantly, more and more deeply, always and forever into our encounter with God. We don't do the liturgical year once, as if it were a practice to be accomplished or a pilgrimage to be experienced. We do the liturgical year over and over again. We do it every year and always so that what we missed in it before this, what we did not have the spiritual development to understand before, we can come to see when we need it most.

The liturgical year is the experience, in the present, of the mysteries of the past and their promise that the reign of God will, someday, eventually, be fulfilled in the future. It is in the liturgical year where we come to realize that time, life, the real world, is where we encounter God. And that is the essential, the engendering, the ultimate adventure of life.

NOTES

Chapter 2

1. Louis Bouyer, *Liturgical Piety* (Notre Dame, IN: University of Notre Dame Press, 1955), 189.

Chapter 3

1. Adolph Adam, *The Liturgical Year, Its History and Its Meaning After the Reform of the Liturgy*, trans. Matthew J. O'Connell (Collegeville, MN: The Liturgical Press, 1990), 70.

Chapter 4

1. Adam, *The Liturgical Year*, 63.
2. Ibid., 121.

Chapter 5

1. Mark Searle, "Sunday: The Heart of the Liturgical Year," in Maxwell E. Johnson, ed., *Between Memory and Hope: Readings on the Liturgical Year* (Collegeville, MN: The Liturgical Press, 2000), 63–64.
2. Ibid.

Chapter 7

1. Alfred Lord Tennyson, "In Memoriam," canto 56, http://home.att.net/~tennysonpoetry/56.htm.

Chapter 8

1. Richard M. Nardone, *The Story of the Christian Year* (New York: Paulist Press, 1991), 20.

Chapter 10

1. Adam, *The Liturgical Year*, 130.
2. Martin J. Connell, "The Origins and Evolution of Advent in the West," in Johnson, *Between Memory and Hope*, 349.

3. Thomas J. Talley, *The Origins of the Liturgical Year*, 2nd edition (Collegeville, MN: The Liturgical Press, 1991), 79.

Chapter 11

1. Allan K. Chalmers, http://www.quoteworld.org/quotes/2619.

Chapter 12

1. Thomas J. Talley, *The Origins of the Liturgical Year*, 97.

Chapter 13

1. Adam, *The Liturgical Year*, 43–44.

Chapter 17

1. Nardone, *The Story of the Christian Year*, 20.
2. Adam, *The Liturgical Year*, 91.
3. Patrick Regan, "The Three Days and the Forty Days," in Johnson, *Between Memory and Hope*, 127.

Chapter 18

1. The International Commission on English in the Liturgy, Inc., *The Sacramentary* (New York: Catholic Book Publishing Co., 1974), 77.

Chapter 19

1. Robert G. Ingersoll, *The Works of Robert G. Ingersoll*, (NY: Dresden, 1900), 98.
2. William Faulkner, *Requiem for a Nun*, (NY: Routledge, 1951), 276.

Chapter 21

1. Regan, "The Three Days and the Forty Days," 126.
2. Ibid.
3. Ibid., 129.
4. Paul F. Bradshaw, "The Origins of Easter," in Johnson, *Between Memory and Hope*, 111.
5. Ibid., 113.

5. Ibid., 113.

Chapter 22
1. Adam, *The Liturgical Year*, 65.

Chapter 23
1. Adam, *The Liturgical Year*, 69.
2. Ibid.

Chapter 25
1. Talley, *The Origins of the Liturgical Year*, 5.
2. Adam, *The Liturgical Year*, 77.
3. Ibid., 59.

Chapter 29
1. Walter Abbott, gen. ed., *The Documents of Vatican II* (New York: The American Press, 1966), 155.
2. Adam, *The Liturgical Year*, 166.
3. Ibid., 177.

Chapter 30
1. Jim Forest, "Dorothy Day—A Saint for Our Age?, The Catholic Worker, http://www.catholicworker.com/cwo002.htm.

Chapter 31
1. Kilian McDonnell, "The Marian Liturgical Tradition," in Johnson, *Between Memory and Hope*, 406.

Chapter 32
1. McDonnell, "The Marian Liturgical Tradition," in Johnson, *Between Memory and Hope*, 400.
2. Pope Paul VI, "Approval of the General Norms for the Liturgical Year and the New General Roman Calendar," http://www.catholic.com/thisrock/1999/9909qq.asp.

ABOUT THE AUTHOR

JOAN CHITTISTER is one of the church's key visionary voices and spiritual leaders. A Benedictine Sister of Erie, Pennsylvania, Sister Joan is an international lecturer and award-winning author of more than thirty-five books.

She is the founder and executive director of Benetvision: a resource and research center for contemporary spirituality located in Erie (www.benetvision.org).

Currently she serves as cochair of the Global Peace Initiative of Women, a partner organization of the United Nations, facilitating a worldwide network of women peace builders, particularly in Israel and Palestine. She is also cochair of the Network of Spiritual Progressives with Rabbi Michael Lerner and Cornel West.

She has appeared on *Meet the Press* with Tim Russert, was interviewed on *NOW* with Bill Moyers and has appeared with the Dali Lama at peace building events. Her commentary from Rome on the month-long coverage of the death of Pope John Paul II and election of Pope Benedict XVI was aired on CNN, the BBC, and all national US media networks.

Sister Joan writes a regular Web column, "From Where I Stand," for the *National Catholic Reporter* and has received numerous awards and recognition for her work for justice, peace, and equality, especially for women in the Church and in society.

Over a half dozen of her books have received awards from the Catholic Press Association.

Sister Joan received her doctorate from Penn State University in speech-communication theory and was an invited fellow and research associate at St. Edmund's College, Cambridge University. She also held the Brueggeman Chair of Ecumenical Theology at Xavier University and has received twelve honorary degrees.

She served as president of the Leadership Conference of Women Religious, president of the Conference of American Benedictine Prioresses for sixteen years, and was prioress of the Benedictine Sisters of Erie for twelve years.

THE ANCIENT PRACTICES SERIES

PHYLLIS TICKLE, GENERAL EDITOR

Finding Our Way Again by Brian McLaren

In Constant Prayer by Robert Benson

Sabbath by Dan B. Allender

Fasting by Scot McKnight

The Sacred Meal by Nora Gallagher

The Liturgical Year by Joan Chittister

*Stand at the crossroads and look; ask for the ancient paths,
ask where the good way is, and walk in it,
and you will find rest for your souls.*
—Jeremiah 6:16 NIV

THOMAS NELSON
Since 1798